Living off the Land

I fondly dedicate this book to the memory of the farmers in my life – my brother Pádraig and my parents Mary Ann and Patrick Russell.
(JR)

I would like to dedicate this book to my family for all their help and support throughout the production of this book.
(LL)

Living off the Land

Women Farmers of Today

Interviews by **Josephine Russell**
Photography & Design by **Lily Lenihan**

CURRACH
PRESS

First published in 2008 by
CURRACH PRESS
55A Spruce Avenue, Stillorgan Industrial Park, Blackrock, Co.
Dublin
www.currach.ie
1 3 5 4 2
Cover and origination by Lily Lenihan
All photography & design by Lily Lenihan

Printed in Ireland by ColourBooks, Baldoyle Industrial Estate,
Dublin 13
ISBN: 978-1-85607-973-0
The authors have asserted their moral rights.

Contents

Introduction

This portrayal of twelve Kerry farming women of various ages between forty and ninety gives a glimpse into the lives of farming women today as well as in times past and will resonate with farming women nationwide. We hear the strong confident voice of the Kerry farming woman with her roots in the past and her eye firmly on the future. It is a random portrayal, a subtle comment on lives at a moment in time. During my conversations with the women they reflected on the lives they lead, the choices they have made and the joys and hardships that are part and parcel of working life on a farm.

The interviews became a journey through time for me. I made my way to farms in easily accessible areas of lush green pastureland and up long bohereens and mountain roads to hilly farms, travelling amid mountains and seascapes through the breathtakingly beautiful Kerry countryside. Over cups of tea and scones in cosy farmhouse kitchens or outside on the farm, sometimes while forking silage, I posed lots of questions and recorded the conversations. Having come from a dairy-farming background myself I was interested in the women's personal history, how they came to be in farming and their level of satisfaction with it. We talked about lifestyle and the upbringing of children, the difficulties of farming in today's changing climate and their hopes for the future. I was interested also in the division of labour and how active a role the women played in management and decision making. Lily Lenihan, who was brought up on a Kerry farm, later came and photographed all the women.

The choice of women was random. Word of mouth recommendations provided many of them and others were suggested by friends. Some had to be persuaded to take part. Lily and I wanted a cross-section of age groups, a cross-section of different types of farming and a spread that included as much regional diversity as possible. In north Kerry I interviewed Marie McEnery and Eleanor Cremins, who are involved in dairying. Nearby in Beal I interviewed Kate Carmody, dairy farmer and cheesemaker, who makes a strong case for organic farming and a return to Slow Food. Noreen Hanafin and Maria O'Connor give an account of dairying and sheep farming in the Dingle peninsula. Further south is Mary Lenihan, also a dairy farmer and keeper of a great variety of animals. Catherine Griffin Lenihan, recently retired from dairying, gives an account of farming through the decades. Farming in times past with all its joys and hardships is outlined by Kitty Doyle of Killorglin and Mary Quilter of Scartaglen. Further west near Waterville Helen Ryan has a suckler herd and is very conscious of where we need to be, keeping our eye on the future. In south Kerry we get a view of sheep farming and its prospects from Rita Foley of Dromid and Breda Lynch of Bunane.

The people we met were open-hearted and friendly with a devilish sense of humour. I was struck by the candour of these women, their vitality and sense of fun, their love of music and dance and their ability to thrive in the face of adversity. They love their work with a passion and some regret that the financial rewards of farming are so meagre that their children would be unlikely to farm as they had done. What you have here are the edited transcripts of those conversations.

The structure of Kerry farming reflects global trends – a decline in the number of full-time farmers and an increase in part-time farming. The portraits of women from early forties to age ninety open a window into modern Ireland and show a remarkable shift from the era of their parents. Fewer children mean that a woman is freer to take up part-time employment outside the home or to be in the thick of the action with her husband on the farm. Farming in Kerry has changed radically from the days when the farmer was king of his own destiny. While Ireland has benefitted hugely from EU membership over several decades there is a price to be paid for prosperity: one consequence is having one's sense of freedom eroded by distant bureaucrats. Dictates from Brussels with an ever-increasing number of new rules and regulations make life more stressful and frustrating now. Some farmers see themselves as being overwhelmed by EU rules. While they may agree with the overall policies many of the women complain that some regulations do not make much sense and involve increased expense for the farmer.

On the other hand prosperity has impacted to a large extent on education, leading to greater self-esteem and sense of identity, although some women for various reasons still feel the need to seek a separate identity outside farming. The women of Celtic Tiger Ireland are generally joint decision-makers and joint owners of the farm holdings, a clear change from the past. There is more shared management, with joint financial control and joint bank accounts. In times of hardship in a less prosperous Ireland these were not the burning issues and one did not argue over management when there was a smaller cake to cut. However some farming women argue that they are worse off since the introduction of PRSI for the self-employed because they cannot make payments in their own right instead becoming the 'dependent spouse' when they reach pension age.

Young women growing up on farms can now aspire to the same chances as their male siblings. There is more equality of opportunity and more equality in relationships between men and women in farming. Yet young women who choose to go into farming are few. I had difficulty in finding women in their twenties and thirties who were willing to be interviewed and was frequently told that there were none. Old traditions die hard and farm practices still tend to favour sons as successors to the family holding. While women are working side by side with their men on the ground it is largely men who avail of agricultural education and training. As yet there is little improvement in the representation of women in farming organisations in Kerry and that is perhaps true of the country as a whole. Irish agriculture is, as one woman termed it, 'the last bastion of male chauvinism'.

One cannot help but be in awe of the strength of the woman in a man's world as these women have had to negotiate their way where the roles are reversed. A woman had to prove herself to be accepted so that men could deal with her on equal terms. Adaptability is the key to survival for those outside dairying, being open to moving into alternative enterprises where a niche can be identified. Many have turned to such enterprises as cheese-making, ice-cream production or farm tourism. Alternatives do not come easily if one has a hill farm that traditionally produces sheep. In a sense one is 'married' to the sheep here. All the women admit that there is little money in sheep farming and one has to suffer the indignity of accepting subsidies instead of achieving an acceptable market price, while watching the middleman getting the lion's share. Many would agree that the whole fabric of rural Ireland with the farm at its centre has changed. Some of the women interviewed thought it a lovely life if one were 'cut out for it' and a wonderful environment for rearing children, but they still made reference to a dying tradition and the unwillingness of modern women to accept the same level of hardship or make the same sacrifices.

Some of the older women described the hardships of farming in their early days, milking by hand with the three-legged stool and ploughing with the horses: 'Times were hard but we were happy.' These same women took to the milking machine with gusto. Electricity was the biggest miracle to hit rural Ireland and many of the older women remember its coming with awe. It revolutionised the lives of women everywhere but particularly rural farm women both inside and outside the home. One could hardly imagine today's woman rearing children without a washing machine, kneeling down on the floor near the tin bath, washing and rinsing clothes by hand. The hardship of rearing big families while one had to be out with cattle and sheep and rushing in to check on a sleeping child or leaving the older ones in charge of the younger siblings is hard to visualise nowadays. The milking machine brought a new dawn to the farming community, freeing up labour and gradually leading to increased stock and a new level of technological expertise. Farming women were not found wanting here. Today's farming women work diligently and are on the whole very well informed on all aspects of farming and technological expertise, have fewer children and can aspire to the highest level of education for their families.

The reality of farming in Kerry today is that only those in full-time dairying depend on it as the sole income. The future prospects for dairying are good as milk prices rise and the EU milk quota system changes, but sheep or beef farming on small holdings is no longer a viable enterprise. Most men and women in such enterprises have to work outside the home to supplement the income. It is not easy to diversify in farming. The nature of the land and the extent of one's holding largely determine one's choices. Farming as we know it will change further still. The booming building trade and high wages for most of the past decade have lured many farming sons away from the farm. Many women referred to the seductiveness of the steady weekly wage and the free weekends in contrast with farming where one is tied seven days a week with much night work involved in the calving or lambing seasons.

Bigger farm holdings and increased prosperity have also brought increased isolation. Many older women remember the camaraderie of the olden days when the farmers brought the milk to the creamery and had an opportunity to chat with their neighbours. The bulk-tank collection has put an end to all that. One has to reach out for social contact and be part of community organisations if one wants to survive in an enterprise where some farmers meet no one outside their own family in the course of the day. In common with most rural dwellers farmers are victims of the new drink-driving laws. The pub was the centre of social activity but the new laws mean that many no longer enjoy a drink because they have to consider driving home and most live in areas where they do not have the benefit of public transport. Big modern pubs dominated by TV have also affected those who prefer the old-fashioned pub where one could have a quiet chat. Many would argue that lack of public transport and the no-smoking laws in public places do not work for the rural population. While technology has improved working conditions, human contact has declined but in some rural areas young people are coming back again to build homes.

The feeling for the Irish language is palpable in many of the women's stories. It no longer occupies a prime position in school as it did in the old days and in the Gaeltacht areas it has to compete with increasing inroads from English. The farming women from the Irish-speaking areas are proud of their knowledge of the language and would love to see it passed on. Increasing interest in Irish is coming from urban areas and from unlikely places abroad. There is increasing demand for Irish language and culture in many American universities which may well fuel a return to the Gaeltacht areas for immersion in the language. It takes an American comedian like Des Bishop to make us sit up and take note of our Irish language heritage again.

Since these portrayals are recorded conversations, the reader may note some unusual forms of oral English such as 'They're sold with a week' or 'I'm happy out'. Many of these expressions are direct translations from Irish that have survived in the oral tradition. I decided to present these stories in the first person so that the idiom and richness of Kerry expressions would be retained. They are arranged in alpabetical order.

This book was a joy to put together and it was both a privilege and a humbling experience to be allowed to enter the worlds of these women. Special thanks are due to Jo O'Donoghue of Currach Press for being supportive and facilitating these portrayals. Others who offered help and advice were Chriss and Danny Nolan, Donie Foley, Carole Hogan, Kathleen O'Gorman and Tom Marren. Go raibh míle maith agaibh uilig!

Josephine Russell
Dublin, July 2008

Kate Carmody

'I make my own type of cheese called 'Beal.'

Kate Carmody (50) is originally from Liverpool. After qualifying as a biochemist she met and married a Kerryman and they had four daughters. Kate is now an organic milk producer and cheesemaker in Beal, near Ballybunion. She has coped with major challenges in her life and is a great example of triumph in the face of adversity.

I grew up in Liverpool, just outside the city. My father was a barrister and a judge and I have two brothers who are lawyers. I have six siblings in all – three brothers and three sisters. I was very privileged. I had wonderful parents who had great open minds and we were dragged around every art gallery, museum, stately home and castle in the north-west of England for our childhood. It gives you a huge appreciation of every aspect of life, especially the heritage of the environment. It is one thing that has been so neglected in this country. I was very aware of it. My mother came from a farming background in Yorkshire. Her aunt had made Wensleydale cheese so that's where the cheese came from. When I got married she gave me a book and a cheese press and said every dairy farmer should make their own cheese. She was a woman very much in touch with arts and crafts.

At university I followed a family tradition. I'm a sixth-generation chemist. My father's father was a chemist. His father-in-law was a chemist, his father and his father – it goes all the way back to 1834. It's quite ironic because my ancestors came from Dublin and formed a chemical company in Liverpool which became part of ICI, which in turn was responsible for all the what I call 'aggressive fertilisers' that are used today. So it's quite ironic that I've gone right round the circle.

We would come here to Ireland on holidays. Every summer we'd come and we loved it. I felt so at home here and when I finished my degree I came to work here. I worked at Cork University Hospital and Nenagh General Hospital and then when I got married I worked in the Bon Secours in Tralee. I met my husband in Ballybunion, the right place to meet a husband! He was incredibly charming and very intelligent even though he had huge health problems. You have to look beyond the veneer of people. He was an amazing man. At first we dabbled in organic farming but he wasn't too keen on it. He was a very intensive dairy farmer. He built up his farm to a great stage. When he got very ill in the 1990s and I took over the farm he was quite happy for me to convert it. He enjoyed it all once it got going. I talked about everything to him and included him in everything.

I've just done my Masters in biomedical science. I finished the exams just before Patrick died. It was a huge personal achievement. I did that as well as doing farming full time and making cheese. That was quite a commitment as well as rearing children and looking after a sick husband. I enjoy life. Life is for living, as I tell the young ones. I've been through all the stages in life where you know sickness and ill-health and I've made my way out of it. You just have to. I went back to work after years because I had children in university and I had to get some more money to keep them. I was doing five days a week in the laboratory plus overtime. I'm going back to work in January and I'll only do three days a week and no overtime for the time being. I've just had more surgery and I don't feel up to punishing myself. I've had thirty-eight operations because I was born with a very severe bilateral cleft palate. It was so severe they actually thought I wouldn't live for the first week. It's very hard to keep me down. I had corrective surgery all through my childhood, all through my teenage years, even going into college.

We tried to involve our four girls in farming but the elder three had no interest. Frances went off and did psychology and biology. She's working in Liverpool now. She went to the university I went to and we're very alike. I think she will stay over there. June, the second girl, is doing languages. She'd make a great lawyer in my opinion. The third girl, Bridget, is interested in social care and Molly, my Irish Molly – she wants to be a part-time farmer and a part-time biochemist. She's very interested in the farm. She was out there all summer. Between us we could manage. Charlie, who works for me, reckons that in two years she'll be ready to milk on her own. She's just like my husband. She'll go round the yard and she has the strength of an ox already. She can pick up my eighteen-year-old and she's only nine. My girls are very much kicking against me at the moment. You know the teenagers/early-adults asserting themselves. They'll go out of their way to say they don't like farming but you can see it rubbing off on them. They appreciate things. I'm hoping that they will appreciate the good side of life because agriculture is a good life.

I run an organic dairy farm, one of only twenty in the Republic of Ireland. The whole farm is sixty-three acres and I rent another couple of farms to bring me up to the level of holding I need to run an efficient operation here. I have quite a large milk quota which I acquired over the years through my cheese business. I'm farming about a hundred and fifty-five acres. We have fifty to seventy cows and we milk all year

'I make cheese in the summer. We use unpasteurised milk here so hygiene has to be the most important factor. Using milk from cows that are out on summer grass is the best because they come in clean to start with.'

round. We supply Glenisk with milk and this is important for them because they need to supply the market all year round. I make cheese in the summer. We use unpasteurised milk here so hygiene has to be the most important factor. Using milk from cows that are out on summer grass is the best because they come in clean to start with. I make my own type of cheese called Beal. It's an unpasteurised territorial-type cheese. I've also started making pasteurised chedder cheese but I actually have to take my milk to another plant to make it because I can't pasteurise here.

> 'We buy an awful lot of organic cereals. It is horrendously expensive because they are nearly twice the price of conventional cereals, all because we don't have enough arable organic farmers in this country.'

Recently my husband died and I'm really farming on my own. Well, I have been since 1997. My husband retired under the Early Retirement Scheme. It's quite unusual that I was so much younger than him and I could take over from him. We'd talk about the farm and discuss everything but he wasn't allowed to work and he wasn't able to work so I ran the farm for the last ten years on my own. But I employ one labour unit through the Farm Relief Service.

I farm differently as an organic farmer. Organic farming is sustainable farming. We create a sustainable system by not using any artificial inputs such as water-soluble fertilisers because they are responsible for destroying so much of our water and they run off very quickly. The ideal system for us is to be totally sustainable where we use our own slurry from the animals and recycle that back on to the land. Most dairy farmers treat it as a waste, not as an asset. We export a lot of our fertility from the farm in terms of milk production and the way we bring it back in is by buying organic cereals to feed the cows. We buy an awful lot of organic cereals. It is horrendously expensive because they are nearly twice the price of conventional cereals, all because we don't have enough arable organic farmers in this country. It's all imported from England and Holland. If organic farming was more widespread it would reduce costs.

For organic farming you have to look at grass differently. You don't produce grass the way you would on conventional farms because you're growing clover as well. Clover is the powerhouse of organic farming. We'd have a much more open sward, which is what the wildlife love. They can move through it. Clover will fix all the nitrogen you require. When you consider artificial fertiliser half of it ends up in the waterways. Another quarter is taken up by the atmosphere. So that's a huge resource being thrown away. We rely on clover. Occasionally we have problems with it. If you get a lot of leatherjackets – the larvae of the daddy longlegs or the crane fly – they will destroy clover. In organic farming you're working with nature and you're not using pesticides. There's nothing artificial there that can influence the animal or the human being unnaturally. You've the added benefits of improving your environment, which is something I feel very strongly about. When we started there were a lot of birds missing from the farm because of intensive agricultural practices and they have all come back now. I have my skylarks. I love them. You could lie in the field and watch them up in the sky. They must be one of the most heartlifting creatures. You know the whole place has come back into life with organic farming. I'm just waiting now for the corncrake. I have a wildlife habitat created in a wet area of the farm and I'm waiting for my corncrake to come. They pass through here on their way up the country so I'm hoping to entice one. Someone said I could put up a sign that says, 'Stop here.' You know I have a great involvement in the environmental safekeeping of the local area. Someone has to mind it.

There were no organic advisers until recently. Teagasc finally appointed three advisers and there are four altogether now. Up to now I've been advising people and Teagasc have referred people to me. I could become a consultant but I don't want to. I'd rather be in touch with the earth. At advisory level a woman is discriminated against although it is very subtle. They don't mind women doing the donkey-work but they won't let them make the decisions. It's possibly male chauvinism that dominates agriculture in Ireland. I think it's the last bastion of male chauvinism and politics might not be far behind.

I'm a director of IOFGA, Irish Organic Farmers Growers Association, which is the largest organic certification body. I'm also a member of the IFA and the ICMSA and they just drive me spare because their idea of women is that they should be feeding the calves or looking after the books. Or would I go on the Farm Women Committee? I will not go on this from the very point of view that they'd be quite happy to relegate me to a little box and I'm a great believer in getting out of the box and pushing people out of the box. People don't like being pushed out of their comfortable little zones. This is the trouble with Irish farm organisations. They get very cushy for the men and women are so lacking in Irish agriculture it's sad. They won't let women become involved. I've gone into houses where men have said no way would they vote for a woman. Most were kind of old but the younger ones would be amused. I'm quite well known for speaking out my mind and people will say if I decide to do something they know that I'll do it. Women aren't really getting involved in agriculture because they're not allowed and because it's male-dominated. I sat at an IFA meeting in Tralee and afterwards I was described as a 'thorny briar'.

I have just put in solar panels and my next goal is to put an anaerobic digester on the farm. It would take all the slurry and organic waste on the farm before it is spread on the fields. I'll take the methane off to heat water or generate electricity. Methane is a potent global warming gas. What I'll be left with then is a liquid fertiliser which is sterile. It will have no weed seeds in it and it can be analysed for N, P and K – you know the nitrogen, phosphate, and potash constituents. And there will also be a sludge which again will be sterile and will have no weed seeds because weed seeds are a big problem in organic grassland. It will be spread like slurry on the ground. To me that is the way to go. That would take a big financial investment of about € 125,000. I'm waiting to see if I can get a grant. This is a sensible project, perfectly feasible, and it will mean that I can take in organic slurry from other organic farmers – and there are a few. It would help them out and it

'In Ireland we think we're big but we're small in terms of agriculture. We were renowned for our good food. We trade on that all the time but you look at the reality of it. You look at the information from the food regulatory database and it's frightening what's in our food.'

would help save the environment.

I've done a REPS [Rural Environment Protection Scheme] course and I've provided this farm as an open farm for various courses for farmers. I did a very interesting course run by LEADER in Tralee the winter before last where they took a group of twenty farmers and introduced all sorts of business and life-skills training. I met a lot of very interesting farmers and we got a discussion going. They are doing another course now to bring us up to another level. When I was at that course

I gave them all a talk on organic farming and the consultant said that I should be a consultant myself. A lot of them were just looking for alternative ideas. You can't afford to stay inside your box any more. You have to get out there and find something. You can't lie down and just give up. It is such a wonderful world and when you live here what more could you have?

My social life has been my involvement in a lot of environmental organisations. I was chairman of the Kerry association of An Taisce for several years but I gave it up the year before last because my husband was so ill. I've been chairman of the Kerry Society for the Prevention of Cruelty to Animals. I'm involved in a new group of organic milk producers where we're setting up a new business so this gives me a social life. I'm off to Mexico to the Slow Food Congress with Darina Allen and Giana Ferguson. Giana does the Gubeen cheese. They are both Trojan women and I like Trojan women. There are five of us. There will be six hundred delegates from all over the world and we'll be looking at the problems facing the indigenous farmers of the world and the way that they are being driven off the land to create space for intensive agriculture. This is very true in countries like India and South America where there is a big drive to plant genetically-modified crops which are probably going to be the downfall of the human race.

Slow Food of course gives me a huge opening for social events in the country and worldwide. It's a whole movement against the globalisation of food and agriculture. What we have happening at the moment is a form of globalised swill being created by global food companies. It's all beginning to

taste the same. And the indigenous farmers, many from the poorer regions as well as in our own country, are being driven out of business in this quest for multinational profit. We're losing the real value of our food which is the taste and the quality and that's what Slow Food is all about – fighting this so that people learn to appreciate where their food comes from. What you eat is what you are. You don't need to be sold a lot of chemicals. You should be able to hunt out locally what you want to eat. We eat our own meat here. I have five freezers. I sell meat as well. I sell sausages and rashers made from our own pigs. I have beef and pork. I sell to a lot of my friends in the hospital.

Organic farming offers a value-added product. We are producing things that people want and they're finding a niche market. The farming organisations say, 'Oh we cannot go by a niche market,' but we can in Ireland. We're small. We think we're big but we're small in terms of agriculture. We were renowned for our good food. We trade on that all the time but you look at the reality of it. You look at the information from the food regulatory database and it's frightening what's in our food. People do not want GM food. The only people who want it are the people with vested interests. People would be better off going to the local farmer's market. There you can get organic farm produce very cheap. If you go into somewhere like Tesco a lot of their organic produce may be 15% dearer but it is not out of the way. People buy too much stuff anyway. If people were more discerning about quality rather than quantity they'd be better off. Food doesn't have to be fancy – good basic home cooking, you know a stew, things like that. People don't know how to cook. They're buying what some call cheap food which is fast. It's only cheap because it's full of wheat or soya fillers. And all these fillers are bad for you. They put weight on you. I don't buy organic bread because it's not available. I buy a local sliced pan. When you live on the periphery of Europe it's a bit hard. I've got organic potatoes there and they're way better than any conventional potatoes. I grew a lot of vegetables here. I've a kitchen full of broad beans. I grew a few potatoes to try them but I think next year I might grow half an acre. I want to try some oats as well for feeding my hens. I keep hens and ducks and I have four sows. Everything is recycled – all food waste, everything.

I keep four sows which I breed but this year they haven't bred at all because we've been so much in a heap with my husband's passing away. I'm in the process of buying a boar so there will be pigs galore here next year. There are very few people producing pigs now, which is a pity. They are very expensive to feed but you know you can't beat the flavour of

'Life is for living, as I tell the
young ones. I've been
through all the stages in life
where you know sickness and
ill-health and I've made my
way out of it. You just have to.'

the meat. The rashers are heavenly. I love pigs. They're ideal on a farm because they'll eat waste milk, waste cheese, anything. You're recycling. My pigs are not in a pig house all day. I built some cottages and they have runs so they can root around. I have to go to a recognised abattoir for pork because they have to be put into boiling water after they are killed. We're lucky that there is a place in Lixnaw but the last lot of pigs I got killed I had to carry them down to Tipperary to Dundrum and I had them made into sausages and rashers and bacon and that's why I have so many freezers. I wouldn't watch them being killed any more. I did when I was younger but not now. But you know I have a consolation they have been well looked after, well fed and I enjoy eating them. Normally I'd put them in the freezer for a week or two before I eat them. I keep hens and ducks as well, all free-range and well fed organically. I love duck eggs. Oh I love them, the yolk. I put them in omelettes as well. I love cooking when I get a chance. I am a good cook. I couldn't not be a good cook when you consider my mother. She taught us the value of good food and we were brought up with it. I enjoy good food. That's why I love organic food. You're sure of not getting chemicals in your food. People are getting a decent price for producing it. The animals are being treated properly. There are so many benefits. The environment is benefiting from organic food and that's a very important message, and it's a message that many people are turning their backs on. I think farming is a great life.

Eleanor Cremins

Eleanor Cremins (43) farms with her husband Brendan in Ballydonoghue, Lisselton. They have four children, two of whom are at home. Eleanor came from an urban background and qualified as a nurse. She got into farming on marrying Brendan. Together they manage a large dairy herd. Now she is an expert on all aspects of dairy husbandry and has IT skills to match.

Farming is a very fulfilling life but if you weren't interested in it, it would be extremely complicated. You need to like what you're doing because you do things that you wouldn't do in other areas. You see things. Things can be very challenging. They can be sad. Sometimes you work hard at something with regard to one particular animal and then you lose that animal. You see everything from birth to death on the farm. You have to learn to deal with every situation and be capable of doing anything from plumbing to veterinary, to basic farming, to the house, to the garden, everything.

We have a Friesian herd. On a typical day we get up about 7.30. We'd have the breakfast and Brendan, my husband, would start bringing in the cows. He'd prepare for the milking while I'd be getting the children organised for school. We have four children. Clare and Jim are away and Emer and Kevin are at home. One is in university and one doing Leaving Cert. The youngest is thirteen. They're picked up outside the door here and taken to school which is wonderful.

When they're gone then I'm up the yard to turn on the computer and get the milking started. We record the yields of the cows on to the computer. All the cows are tagged and they have an extra tag so that they will be read when they are going into the milking parlour. If we have any problem cow we can enter it on the computer and the following morning it confirms that there is a problem and gives a warning to beware. I do all the computer side of it. Brendan wouldn't be wonderful at that. I talk him through it but he'll come back the next day and say, 'You do it.' I have internet access via broadband. I think it is essential. I must admit I like the computer, not just the programs but I like the technical aspects of it as well. I like to be able to put them together myself and know what's wrong and if there is a problem. Sometimes I get help from my brother-in-law in Farranfore. There is connectivity to the computer through the mobile phone but I don't use it. We have it if we want to. If we were away we could ring and get details of how the cows were milking and things like that. I don't know anybody here who uses it but I know it is widely used in the north of Ireland. We're always here so we don't need to use it. Brendan says that when he gets away he likes to turn off completely from the farm and deal with the situation when he comes back.

We have always had a pedigree herd and when I came here initially it was an absolute nightmare trying to find out what exactly was going on. I knew nothing about farming. I had done nursing. I had no experience of farming. I had an uncle who was a farmer and I was on holiday at his farm once or twice but it was purely fun. When I came to this pedigree herd we had to start registering all the animals and every year you'd have to go back on records. It was complicated work, a nightmare. Eventually I heard that there was a computer program that would help me with this but I had to learn how to use the computer. I contacted the Irish Farm Computers who do this particular program that I use and they showed

me how to use it. It made life a lot easier with regard to registration. At the moment we milk around seventy cows, all Friesian. Most of what we have is our own stock that we've reared. The only outsiders are two bulls and everything else that's on the farm is reared here. Brendan does AI (artificial insemination) himself. He did a course for that many years ago and was probably one of the first in the area to start it.

Brendan would make most of the decisions with regard to the farming side of things. I'd probably make more of them with regard to the children. I didn't take as much an interest in the early years but Brendan had a health problem back in the mid-1990s and I had to muck in then and keep things running and thanks be to God he got over that. He's in full action now and we work hand-in-hand milking, morning and evening, every day. We had help some time ago but we found it complicated with the children here as well. Life is nicer when there's nobody extra living around. We had a chap and he took off on holiday and never came back. We have never replaced him since.

We were very intensive but the new nitrate regulations have affected us and we have had to reduce our stock. We can see they're for everybody's good. We try as best we can to keep up and do something every year to improve the farm. For instance this year we're putting in an aeration system in the slurry tanks. Again it's to do with the environment. It's to reduce the emissions and smell of the slurry and make it less cumbersome workwise. It is a big financial investment but we hope that in the long run it will be labour-saving. The aeration system is a series of pipes in the underground tanks and it blows air through the slurry and keeps it agitated and more liquid. You can then take slurry out at any stage. You're allowed to spread slurry now only during certain periods of the year and you have to stick to that regime. Unfortunately it is farming by dates which I don't think works but the EU would have it that way. You have to be able to avail of the weather. This year we had a bad early summer with constant rain and if farmers wanted to put out the slurry they couldn't because the land wasn't negotiable. If you broke those regulations you'd be fined. Your direct farm payment that you get from the EU could be affected by it.

All the improvements we have made on the farm have been to make things easier because in the springtime Brendan and I are working twelve to fourteen hours a day. And we're out a lot of the time. This time of the year is our quietest – from the end of the summer, from August to November. Then from the 1 January you really have to get down to it until June. We have the cows calving from January. The really heavy period is from January to April and then you're trying to get your cows back in calf and that's difficult enough. We mostly use AI. When we want to spot an animal that's bulling (looking for the bull) we tail-paint the cows to try and pick them up. When they jump up on one another they knock the paint off. Then you know that when an animal hasn't got paint she's possibly bulling and there are other signs as well. They'd have AI within twelve hours of that and we've put a lot of work into that.

The calves are hard work but last year we sold all our bull calves. Because of the new directives we have to. We just have to keep the females now. We might keep one or two extra bulls of good pedigree to sell on at a later date and we'd register

'I tell my children that everything you do
has a different language ... There is a
language in farming.'

them. When you register them you have to send off a DNA sample to make sure that they are who they say they are. I take hair samples and send them off to Wetherbys in Kildare. They do the sampling of the DNA and it is sent back to the Friesian breeders in Clonakilty. They then issue the certificate. Everything is kept above board.

'My nursing training was extremely useful for everything. I have great understanding of what goes on with regard to the health of the animals.'

We don't have a lot of time for holidays. Brendan and I went away to Majorca. The two boys, Jim and Kevin, looked after the farm this year when we had gone. They're able to take over. Jim has done the Leaving Cert and it looks as if he's going to do something in agriculture. No matter what area you're in today you need education. I think it is so important even for the management side of farming. You have to be au fait with what's going on in order to make right decisions because a mistake is costly. Sometimes if you were leaving here and had someone else in charge, you'd be concerned if you had an animal with antibiotic milk. If you hadn't your animal identified properly the milk could go into the tank. The whole tank of milk would go to the creamery and you'd get fined. It has never happened to us but it could happen. If you're caught for that not alone are you fined for your own milk but you're fined for the lorryload of milk. You have to wait a while before sending in that cow's milk if she's been treated with an antibiotic. If you're selling an animal to the factory there's a withdrawal period there as well. Most people abide by those rules for health and safety reasons. You have to be consumer-conscious. Health and safety is a huge issue on the farm. Brendan has been to a lot of meetings with regard to it. His father was always extremely safety-conscious. If he saw something out of place above, looking dangerous, a big tyre leaning in the wrong direction, he'd be down straight away.

My father-in-law and mother-in-law live here. They have their own premises and we have ours but we use the same kitchen. We dine together and we get on great. It was very good having my in-laws living with us when the children were smaller. They'd pick them up from school, bring them to football and bring them home. You were not under such pressure. You'd have Brendan calling you for something up the yard. Farming is not a job for one. You need two. It is extremely difficult for someone to be on their own, even if it is only about standing in a gap. For instance this morning he was putting down those pipes and I was up with him for about an hour handing stuff down to him. We share the work the whole time.

I didn't have a farming background at all. I'm from Birr, County Offaly, from the middle of the town. When I came to Kerry I never thought that I'd wear out so many pairs of wellies. My mother would be amazed to see me. My father and mother had a drapery shop in Connacht Street in Birr. They were both originally from Ballinasloe. My mother was a psychiatric nurse in St Brigid's and my father did an apprenticeship in Cullen's shop in Ballinasloe. We had no land

'Another thing that always intrigued me when I came
first was when they'd say, "there's a cow sick."
... I never realised that when they said the cow
was sick meant that the cow was in labour.'

at all in Birr and you wouldn't be talking too much about land. You wouldn't realise how big an issue land is and how families can have awful disputes and how deep and how vicious and how miserable things can be over land.

I had an uncle, Fr Mannix Hanniffy, who was principal of Pallaskenry Agricultural College for many years. A lot of Kerry folk would have gone through his hands. Other than that I knew very little about farming. When I came first I never realised that the cows were put into a different paddock every day. I had no idea about the grass management side of things. Grass management is an art. Another thing that always intrigued me when I came first was when they'd say, 'There's a cow sick.' Well, to me something sick has a pain in their belly but I never realised that when they said the cow was sick it meant that the cow was in labour. It took me a while. I tell the children that everything you do has a different language. When you go to school your geography has a language. Science has a language. You've got to get used to the language. One way to get used to the language of the subject is to read the textbooks. There's a language in farming. I'd read the *Farming Independent* and *Today's Farm* and the *Furrow*. I'd be interested but I probably wouldn't do enough of it.

I was trained as a nurse. I trained in Liverpool and did my midwifery in Scotland. I had to give up nursing completely when Clare was born. I had intended going back but it just didn't work out. Clare is the eldest and she's nineteen now. I never went back after that. My nursing training was extremely useful for everything. I have a great understanding of what goes on with regard to the health of the animals. I'd know a lot of the drugs. I'd pick up the bottles and I'd be reading the constituents.

I met my husband Brendan when I was working in Tralee. We met just by coincidence one night. I can remember the night well. There were four of us living in the house and Hannah Broderick arrived looking for somebody to go out with her. I was the only one available so we went down to Horan's dance hall and that was the night I met him. We go out now once a week if we can. In the early years when the kids were young we didn't get out much at all. On Saturday night we cross the road to The Thatch and in the summertime we might go to Ballybunion. We wouldn't be socialising a lot. I was never one for the fashion myself. Once I'm half reasonable I'm grand. I like nice things but I wouldn't go overboard.

Brendan pays into a pension scheme. I wouldn't think most farmers do. Physical health is number one for farmers. It has to be because the hardest time on a farm is when one of you is knocked out and the other has to pick up the pieces. Invariably it's in the wintertime when the weather is bad, the days are short and everything is against you. If there are two of you knocked out then you have major problems. It does happen. You get a bad flu and you just cannot physically go up the yard. I can remember last year on a Sunday morning Brendan was not feeling well and Jim came up with me and we started the cows. Next thing I heard a bang outside and I looked out and I saw this cow jumping over a sharp pole. I knew straight away there was something wrong here. I could see the dribble of blood so I was out the door like the clappers and over the gate to stop her. I immediately herded her back in, got her straight up the crush to inspect the damage and I saw she was haemorrhaging. She had cut the milk vein and was pouring blood. So I grabbed the spot that she was haemorrhaging from and held it as best I could to stop the bleeding. I rang the vet because this needed to be sutured properly and we hadn't the equipment. I sat there for half an hour and held the vein until the vet arrived. If we could have done it ourselves we would have. When the vet calls it's usually about a big problem. If we had let the cow out she'd be dead in fifteen minutes. It is so easy to lose a beast. I can remember one morning we went up and this beautiful heifer that we were minding was stone dead. She wasn't milking but what happened to her – well we haven't a clue. She might have got a heart attack. You have casualties and losses. If we can prevent some disease we'll do so rather than trying to treat it.

'Market forces will decide the future for farming. It isn't that easy for farmers to adapt to something else.'

The milk quota system is crazy but it is a necessary evil that will probably be gone in another few years. There's going to be a big demand for milk and what will happen then is that you'll be paid a market price. At the moment there are still subsidies. Market forces will decide the future for farming. It isn't that easy for farmers to adapt to something else. Brendan is in his forties now and is farming since he was knee-high to a grasshopper and he knows no life other than farming. He has done various courses. He did the Green Cert and this would have been the very start of these courses. He went to another farm for a couple of months down in Cork, the best experience of his life. I think it is necessary to see how other people do things. You see things that you wouldn't even think of doing yourself. The Kerry Friesian breeders organise a tour where all the boys go off and visit other farms in various parts of the country. They pick a different area every year. I might be left doing the milking that day.

Teagasc is a great advisory service. They put you in touch with someone who can give you information. Of course the internet now is handy. Some farmers really make use of it. I think not alone are farmers changing but farmers are going to make others change. Every area will have to be more competitive. A lot of people dealing with farmers are closed shops where they have little cartels. Prices are set and the middlemen are creaming off. I think that day is gone. At the moment you can see the milk price is rising. While the farmer is getting a mild increase the retailers are getting a bigger increase. Definitely the margins should be bigger for the primary producer. The speculator is taking over. For a lot of farmers if they want to increase they have to get extra land and with current prices it is extremely difficult to increase the holding. With rules and regulations you can only produce to a certain level. There are huge limits to expansion and the land here is not suitable for crop production. It is heavy soil. As a result of the Tiger economy you have people with extra cash. They are the high-flyers, non-farmers and speculators and land is an investment for them. The value of land never goes down really. It appreciates in value the whole time.

If my son goes into farming he will have to go in with a different attitude. He'll probably have to go away for a while and see what other ideas he can get. You have the likes of Kate Carmody who has gone into the cheese. Maybe that's the way we should be going. Diversify and go into extra activities. Have the milking cows as one part and alternatives like ice-cream production as another. You'd have to research the market and see what the niches are. Well, I think that's the way the future will go for the smaller farmer anyway. At the moment a hundred acres is viable but how long more is that going to be so? That's the question. We'd be coming into that bracket. Unless you diversify and get activities going in the long run it may not be viable. If either of the two boys wanted to leave farming and do something else I wouldn't be in the least bit perturbed about it. I wouldn't think it would bother

Brendan either once they were happy at what they were doing and they were able to do it. To me that is success, that's what life is about. What more do you want out of life?

'If either of the boys wanted
to leave farming and do
something else I wouldn't
be in the least bit perturbed about it ...
once they were happy at what they were doing
... to me that is success,
that's what life is about.'

Kitty Doyle

Kitty Doyle, (76), from Dromin in the parish of Killorglin, has seen many changes in her time, from milking by hand in the era before electricity to the modern era of machines for everything. She raised nine children on her farm without ever having the convenience of a motor car. Kitty drove a tractor but didn't ever drive a car.

I started school at the end of the 1930s. There were six girls of us and I had no brothers. We walked down to the country school in Carnafella. It would be an old-fashioned two-roomed school, big rooms and big fires in the winter, heating our cocoa in bottles by the fire. Some people brought turf to school but not us. We brought money for turf because we were too far away. We couldn't be drawing it down. After finishing in sixth class I went to the technical school for two years. We did the primary certificate that time. There was a secondary school in Milltown as well. My sister went there. All the rest of us went to the technical school. We were fourteen going in. We were a bit older than they'd be now. I had a very bad start there. They didn't send me for two weeks after the opening date. They kept me at home to pick the potatoes. It wasn't a great start going to a new school. That was September and I had to stay at home to sort the potatoes and put them into a pit. My father would be ploughing out drill by drill with a plough. I was mad out. They kept me at home for a full fortnight and then there were ones telling me in school, 'Oh, we know how to thread a sewing machine.' They were teasing me of course about all they learned in that fortnight. I thought I'd never catch up. Of course I did learn to thread a sewing machine and I passed my exams flying in the sewing. One year I had to cut out a nightdress and tack it together and do the seams, another time a blouse. I did a child's dress another time.

We did cooking as well as Irish, English, Maths and Botany. We'd be out in the garden with poor Mr Callanan. He'd have us weeding on a Thursday. There was a big school garden then and it had vegetables and flowers and everything. It's a pity now there are all these houses and flats in its place and there's another vocational school there. I doubt if they go out in the garden now.

We were born and reared in the country and we were used to it and we would cycle back to town to school and Masses. We weren't frightened by the weather. We had to go out in it. And then my mother would have the donkey and cart sometimes going to the creamery. My father would go with the horse. There were two of us going to the tech and we had only one bicycle and one of us would have to go with my mother. The creature – we tormented her to hurry on in case we'd be late. She'd be taking the milk in the tanks with the donkey and of course it was too slow for us. We'd give her an awful time. Well, my mother didn't always have to go. She went when my father was busy. We were made do a lot of work since we had no brother and my father was fairly old. We did our bit setting the potatoes, picking them and saving the hay. We were always off in the hayfields making the wynds and turning the hay. We had no modern machinery. And the same with the corn, we had to bind it. We didn't have to work before we went to school. We were lucky like that, except if something was wrong we might milk a cow. All the milking was done by hand. I would do the milking in the evening. We would milk three or four each. I was considered a good milker. I was the youngest of them of course.

We had a few tanks going to the creamery. You'd empty and strain the milk into the tanks and try to keep it cool. There were no electric coolers that time. To keep it cool we had a well up in the old farmyard above and we'd put the tanks into it. My father would lift them up and put them on a bit of a platform and then they'd take them to the creamery. A man would have to throw it in at the creamery for you. And you'd have the creamery mix then. That was watery buttermilk and they would fatten pigs with it. Sometimes people at the bridge would be out and stop you for a gallon or half a gallon. They'd keep it for making bread. It was a great place for people to meet each other, not like now. The creamery is not there at all of course now.

When we were young we had to feed the pigs and in the springtime we'd be feeding the calves. We fed them buckets of milk. We'd be constantly driving them in and out. We saved wheat and barley, set potatoes and brought the cows for a drink every day. The ploughing was done with two horses and my uncle would do that. In my younger time we had a lot of fowl, geese and turkeys and we'd sell them every Christmas. My mother sold eggs in town. Women had to have some little help that time. She'd sell geese every Christmas. We loved that day out too. They'd have market day a couple of weeks before Christmas. The atmosphere was lovely. I can still remember it in Killorglin. We'd queue up and we'd have what geese we could manage in an old darkened rail. Geese came a few years before the turkeys. We had black turkeys in later years. The town would be packed for the market. There were so many lorries parked in different places. There was one local buyer

'We only had the small milking machine, one of the push ones. The early days were hard ... milking and trying to rear children as well. I had to depend on the bigger ones to watch the smaller ones while we were milking and it was rough.'

from Milltown and buyers also came from Limerick and Cork. There would be all live fowl on sale. We would weigh them at home and tie their legs. We loved that day. It was like going to town for the Christmas.

We'd have goose for Christmas. I hadn't a goose since I was a child now. I think I'd love it. They say there isn't much in them. It was our own goose that we ate. My father would do the killing. My father was great. He'd kill pigs and he'd do it for all the neighbours and then they'd give round the black pudding and the pork to the neighbours. When he was getting old he'd pick one of the younger men. We always reared and killed our own pig. They'd collect the blood in buckets and my mother would make the puddings then. They filled them with the blood and added pinhead oatenmeal and onions and flavouring and then put them in a big pot on an open fire to boil them. You'd have them hanging on the handle of a brush. It was dangerous too wasn't it with all the children? And yet there weren't that many accidents, thanks be to God. Those puddings were lovely. I'd say no one does it now. Even in my early days when I married I didn't. You'd think I'd have continued. I suppose we were starting to go to shops more that time.

In my father's time now growing up you'd cut the hay one day and if the weather was very warm and hot it would be ready to turn the next day. It might take a few days. We had the three-prong pikes. We hated going into the big field at first. They'd make grass cocks in case the rain might come. And then they'd gather it up for wynds. We'd have a horse and an old rake. I didn't ever work with the horse. You'd draw in the wynds with a hay-car. It had a kind of pulley. The whole family would be out then for drives in the hay-car. It was great fun. It was tough enough inside in a warm hayshed. They'd be throwing up the hay and you had to take it back and trample it and pack it. It would always be dry that time whatever was in the weather. We never had bad hay. We loved tea out in the meadow. We'd always be arguing. We all wanted to volunteer to go in to get the tea. It was a hard job getting the fire going with sticks.

'We'd have goose for christmas. I hadn't a goose since I was a child now. I think I'd love it... it was our own goose that we ate.'

When I finished school I went working back in town. I was there for some years. I always meant to go nursing but my father died in the meantime. I think I was nineteen. We gave up the farming then and my mother sold the horse. We were crying after the horse. I stayed on and for a few years I was working in a bar in Killorglin. I served the drink and pulled the pints. I was supposed to be good at that too. I'd to be quick and I'd be in no one's way inside the counter. The owner was there and there were two men there too. I stayed at that until I married. My husband's family had a pub as well at the top of the town. I met my husband at Lyons's dance hall in Killorglin which had dances once a month that time. We all started off in Lyons's I'd say, everyone. We had the Oisín cinema and the more mature boys and girls went to the cinema. Sure I remember Clark Gable and Stewart Granger and Deborah Kerr. I can still picture her. Well, they are all dead now.

When we were going out together we'd go to plays. Travelling theatre companies would come from Dublin for a week now and again once or twice a year. I remember Anew McMaster. In fact the actors would stay where I was working sometimes. I was going out with my husband for maybe two to three years and there were all boys in his family and all girls in our family. We married and we stayed behind in the pub then but my husband never owned it. It belonged to his other brother and eventually it was sold. It isn't there at all now. We went to London for a while. We had two children going to school when we went to London. They were born here at home. We weren't long there, not even a year. We lived in Melbourne Road, Kilburn. I loved it and I'd have stayed there but my mother got lonesome and she begged us to come home. My sisters were all grown up. I was happy out over there but my husband said, 'Think of the future. The children would be better off reared in the country.' Well he was right there. The children were all born at home here, in the hospital in Killarney.

We came back to rear the children in Ireland and he was right when I think about it. I have nine children altogether, three boys and six girls. We came back to the old house where my mother was and then we got this house built by the council. The stock was gone off the farm. My mother had sold everything out. We had to come back and start again. That was tough, very tough. We even had to buy the pony and cart to go to the creamery and start off with so many cows first and build it up bit by bit but we never had a big farm. We only had the small milking machine, one of the the push ones. The early days milking and trying to rear children as well were hard. When there were a lot of them then I had to depend on the bigger ones to watch the smaller ones while we were milking and it was rough. Oh God, there were often accidents. We had to bring one of them to the doctor for stitches in her forehead. She fell against a stone. That was risky and then sometimes when they were going to school I would take a chance and leave a child or two there in bed and run up to wash the tanks and I shouldn't have. It was very difficult to supervise. I had nine children and I was out farming and milking as well as keeping hens and chickens.

It was in the 1950s that we got electricity. Here in this area we weren't bad. It was much later in other places. I remember when the electricity first came. Sure we were delighted. Not everyone got it. Some were old-fashioned. I suppose they thought it would be too dear. Naturally they got it years after. I think they had to pay more then for the poles. It was a big change in the house. Sure before that we'd have to put in the iron in the fire and heat it and then throw salt on it to get the dirt off. And then we had the electric iron and everything was electric. It was a miracle. I remember the radio. We had the old wet batteries and you'd get them recharged. The radio and batteries would take up all the width of the window. The light made a huge difference. Up to then we had a good lamp for a few years. I think it was an Aladdin lamp and it used oil. Before that we had the ordinary lamp up on the wall with a wick but the Aladdin was a big improvement then. It was like a lantern really. There was a cover on it. I remember my mother selling it afterwards to someone who hadn't electricity. We got the iron and the kettle kind of quick. I got the washing machine here later.

When I was young we'd do the washing every Monday with the washing board in a big bath of suds. That was hard work but we were used to it. I suppose it was great exercise. I got my first washing machine down here in this house. It was not automatic. You had to transfer the washing from one place to another and then squeeze it up. There was more work in them than the modern ones. It was more economical because you could use that water again. Now with the automatic washing machine the good clean suds go out don't they? It wouldn't happen at all in that time. When I was rearing my children I washed by hand at the start. I would kneel down on the floor near the bath and I was happy out putting them in water in the bath and rinsing them again. It's funny when you haven't a thing you'd be content. I remember my first fridge but keeping things cool without a fridge wasn't a problem. We hadn't to worry about milk. We had our own milk morning and night and I suppose we'd use a lot of bacon and only buy fresh meat when we were at Mass or in town. You'd eat the meat the next day. It wasn't that much of a problem. If we bought a pound of sausages we'd have to use them quickly of course.

'It's funny when you haven't a thing you'd be content. I remember my first fridge but keeping things cool without a fridge wasn't a problem. We hadn't to worry about milk.'

When the children were small I had no one to mind them during the day. I'd have to wait until the older ones came home. I had to go to Milltown, two and a half miles away, for a few years. I never learned to drive a car and that was a mistake. Wouldn't it be great now if I had? I lost the chance. I tried to learn in later years but I was too nervous and didn't continue. We reared nine children without a car. When we

came home from England we'd get a taxi to bring them all to Mass on Sundays. I'd get good value out of it. The taxi would wait until we came out. They'd buy their ice-cream and a few sweets and they'd be all pleased. I had to give them a lot of pocket money then. The children's allowance was there. We'd cycle as well. My husband drove a car before he got married. He was an inseminator for a bit. Well I suppose he wasn't interested in getting a car. We always had a horse and a donkey as well. My husband is dead since 1988 and we didn't sell the horse when he died. Pádraig continued for a small bit. He'd bring the groceries with the horse.

'They'd make grass cocks in case the rain might come. And then they'd gather it up for wynds. We'd have a horse and an old rake.'

You didn't send for the doctor as much then. Now they are always going to the doctor. We'd send for the vet like everyone else if there was a cow in difficulties calving. I didn't ever deliver a calf on my own but my God I would be there in the process. The slippery legs – you'd have to catch them and pull. God I wouldn't do it now. You'd tie a rope to the calf if it was slow in coming. They say it's not the best thing to do. You'd send for a neighbour too if the cow was very slow. There were great neighbours then. They'd help you out. We had a bull a few times which I wasn't happy about. We used the AI man but we kept our own bull to watch them and put them in calf in case you'd miss them. It was kind of dangerous going out in the field with the bull. Well, I was not so happy about it. My mother would pray. She got very nervous one day and she closed the door and wouldn't open it. I think the bull broke out. You'd be very afraid of a bull.

My husband would make the big decisions on the farm but he'd always leave the money matters to me to pay anyone or anything. There weren't many decisions to make really. If he was buying cattle or different cows he'd do that himself. He'd know the right time. He'd have to look for a lorry if he had a lot of animals to sell but he'd bring the calves down in the tractor and trailer. He'd drive a tractor all right. I drove around the fields there too. It is very easy to drive a tractor. I should have continued that too. My son has the land now. He is thirty-eight and a carpenter. The quota wasn't big enough and we have the farm rented out now. You'd want a big milk quota now to make a living.

I might be wrong but I can't imagine the modern woman doing farm work like I did. I doubt if they go out in the cowhouse at all. Well they don't go into the fields anyway because there's no work in the fields for them. Sure it's done by machinery. Well they'd tell you they haven't an easier life. Sure they're all working and they have to try to balance it to stay with the children. I know my daughters in the city work very hard trying to mind children. If I were starting all over again I wouldn't be going out the fields working. It was too much hardship. I think women have enough to do inside in the house. Modern farming women all have a job. They shouldn't be criticised by older people for not doing their bit.

It was different long ago. They had to be helping to feed the calves and everything.

People are more isolated now without a doubt. We'd go to the creamery and we'd be going in and out. Even the shopkeepers would talk to you that time. There are no small shopkeepers now. With nine children we didn't have much opportunity to go out. There was the odd wedding. That was a guaranteed outing. I'd go out with my sister. Now and again we'd go to the dancing pubs. I liked dancing. I'd dance the waltz, the quickstep and the polka but I wasn't very good at it. My husband wasn't a great dancer but he would dance. In those dances you could dance with everybody else. It didn't matter. In the polkas and the sets you had a change of partners. I can't dance now. I got my knee done last February. Sure I have a stick now, a crutch. I have arthritis in my back and there's nothing they can do about that.

'If I were starting all over again I wouldn't be going out the fields working. It was too much hardship. I think women have enough to do inside the house.'

I go to the day centre in Killorglin on Thursdays. They have a bus and you get picked up from different places. We go in and we have our cup of tea and a home-made scone and chat around with everyone and pick up the papers if we want to. We have bingo in the afternoon. We do the exercises then, not very strenuous, behind a chair when we're standing. We have a lovely dinner and more chat. They have music once a month. I love it and we get all the news. Well I'm great at knowing people. You could go every day if you had your own transport.

Religion and faith played a much stronger part when I was younger. We'd have the stations in our turn. I'd say I was the last in Drumin to have them in the year 2000. They dropped away then. In some parts of north Kerry they still have them. No one in our locality would have them now. The younger people don't and they have the nice houses. Well I suppose they started long ago when people weren't going out much and had to go to Confession. That is done with now with cars being everywhere, not that they go to Confession anyway. It satisfied a need one time. People don't go to Church as much now. Well people like me, the older generation, go but it would amaze you the way they all come back for christenings and getting married. It goes full circle. That's the way. Things have changed anyway.

Rita Foley

Rita Foley (41) farms sheep and cattle in Dromid near Waterville. She is totally passionate about what she does whether it is donning the wellies to fork silage to her cattle or stepping out in high stilettos for socialising and shopping trips to fashion hot-spots.

I will always be a true Kerrywoman, proud of my Kerry accent. There is a perception of farming women as non-glamorous and not even having the opportunity to dress up and socialise. I feel good dressing up after a day in the wellies. I can totally detach from the day job. I always try to keep my hands groomed and I love painting my nails. I make sure that I attend a good hairdresser and have my hair well looked after. Good casual clothes always appealed to me and I have used my mother's designer clothes for special functions. Since my make-over with *Off the Rails* [RTÉ fashion programme] I have taken more of an interest in clothes with more feminine allure. When I wear my red satin dress now every woman hangs on to her man! I have about twenty pairs of stiletto shoes and a massive interest in handbags. En route to Australia shortly I'm going to do some shopping in Singapore and have some dresses made there. Every lamb and calf is hitting the mart to pay for this shopping spree!

I went to the sheep mart in Milltown today and I would usually be the only woman there. I was born and reared with sheep and I'd be able to gauge the lambs that were there with our own and I'd have a fair idea of the price that they should make. Aertel on the television gives us the prices at the marts but there's nothing like going in and seeing what's going through. We kind of grew into this farming. My husband came from a farming background and he went to college in

Pallaskenry. We learned from other people as well. My neighbour and Marie Lenihan next door have taught me an awful lot about calf-rearing. People like that have great ideas about how to manage calves, very simple remedies for ailments that you wouldn't really need the vet for. If a sheep was having problems lambing I could manage that fine. When it comes to a cow I'd be more fearful. I'd have to call one of my brothers or a neighbour. If things went to a crazy state altogether I'd bring the vet out as well.

Donie, my husband, does all the bookwork. All I know is when the bank account is full and there's plenty of money there to spend! Now we have set up a special account and the money from the farm is going into it. It is just to let me really see how much it's making. It pays for my education, my freedom to rear my children and I suppose it gives me something to do. We have an accountant to do the accounts but Donie keeps everything upstairs and he did the computer course. We just give everything in to the accountant and he manages it very well.

My older boy Dónal is now thirteen. He's in first year in secondary school at St Brendan's and he's very caring with the animals. He'd feed them all and when we're down here on a Saturday morning he'd get up and he'd have everything done. We seem to rely more on Dónal but John is very capable as well. He's coming up eleven so he's partaking now and getting very active. They'd both feed the sheep and look after everything. They have an interest in farming and they'd pick the stones out there in the field with their father. They'd spend summer out there on the holidays working away and doing jobs. We line up jobs for them because I think they're away better down here doing any bit of a job than being around the streets of Killarney. We go to the cinema a couple of times a year. We are social people and we go out a lot but I suppose this is our first priority. The contact with animals has given the children a massive understanding and value system. They love taking people around and showing them all the different animals. They love the freedom of it. This year we had a Spanish and a French visitor. They were totally amazed at the vastness of the place.

I don't have any vision of my sons becoming full-time farmers in south Kerry because I don't think there would be a viable income from it but I would see them maybe maintaining it as a side income or as a side interest. For farming to be full-time the standard of living would be very low from the type of farming that we're doing. It's more of a sideline. It's ideally suited for me with the kids at school. It allows me the freedom to be my own boss, to be employed and to manage my time around it. I can arrange my schedule around the child-rearing. If one of the children is sick in the morning I can stay and mind him or I can take him with me in the car to the farm but if I were in another job I would have to be in there at nine o'clock. I gave up my nine-to-five pensionable job at a time when we were just expanding the farm. It had become very repetitive and wasn't fulfilling all my needs or my interests. To have become self-employed as a farmer has been brilliant. I can manage my own hours, manage my own business, and I have it set up now in a way that I have an income out of it. We're investing back into the place all the time to make it more valuable.

You can have such peace except when things go wrong,

'We're fine fit-looking people
and I think a lot of it is
because we're eating our own
food. We have no growth promoters.
We have pure natural Kerry
    mountain sheep.'

when you hear animals bellowing or something like that. One Sunday afternoon a heifer got stuck inside a drain and we could see her but she couldn't come out because she must have been about eight feet down. We knew she was very much trapped inside in the gully. We had an awful job trying to arrange a digger but we finally got this fellow Brian Mills to come up with a digger and he dug her out. It was great because my neighbours all rallied around to help and the animal survived. We had a plan made to go out that day and have a great day in town and it fell totally apart. That can happen with animals any time of course. It is unpredictable.

I met my husband Donie at a dance in Killarney and we travelled to Australia together. Then we came back and got married. We inherited this farm from my uncle Seán in Comastow in Dromid parish near Waterville. It is part of the south Kerry Gaeltacht. I've been farming eight years full-time since I gave up my work. I trained first as a chef and I was student of the year when I finished my training. I had a permanent job Monday to Friday as chief instructor. Then I came down here to take on running the farm. I was reared on a farm but I still didn't know what to do here. I always remember Dad saying, 'Oh Rita won't manage that.' I think that gave me more of an incentive to stick with it. God rest his soul. Everybody has to get into their own system of work. I had great systems devised from being an instructor of training and I set things up very conveniently and efficiently to run like a factory process. I'd stop off in the morning, fill my troughs and I'd let out one lot of sheep. I'd go over to the shed and I'd start another process going there when I'd be feeding the calves. I'd come back then and I'd be feeding another lot of sheep. It's away better than feeding people because as a chef you are only as good as the last meal you put out but these lads will eat anything! We inherited the place at the time I was expecting my first son. At the time it seemed so hard to have to turn around and travel up and down to the farm, an hour-and-a-half drive from home. Now it has become part of life to travel from Kilcummin all the way down to Dromid. We're both very interested in farming and it brings us together more because we're sharing the same interest. There's fantastic satisfaction in going down and seeing our calves inside in the shed being fattened.

'The contact with animals has given the children a massive understanding and value system!'

We're now down here in a place called the Shlough and we're looking at the thirteen cows. We've taken the calves and housed them in the shed to fatten them for the mart and we're going through the cows just to see how they are drying up after the calves have been weaned from them. They're in very coarse rough ground now because they're not going to eat as much to produce milk. It's a kind of a fasting period and there's one I'm concerned about. She's lost two paps with mastitis so it would have been a big concern to watch her drying off this year. Her ears are up which is a good sign. She's

feeding and chewing the cud. All the others seem to be fine
and content. You'd know the sadness in them since the calves
have been taken away.

The calves are taken away now with about two weeks and
they're housed inside and we're feeding them with ration and
silage and some hay. These cows will be put in as the weather
gets bad. We'll move them up to another bit of coarse ground
and we'll bring them in and feed them for the winter. We have
kept the bull now from some of these cows because we want
to have later calving. If you have a stronger calf you're going
to have fewer problems and they make more money in the
mart as well. You'd be talking maybe of an August sale and
they'd be better calves.

We don't send for the vet a lot really. They're healthy
enough as a rule. A thing would have to be very bad here for
the vet to come. To treat mastitis you can put in tubes yourself
and milk them out but if they get chronic mastitis the vet has
to come out. We had a case when that black cow there got
chronic mastitis and lost her paps. It had gone into the blood,
into the bone. She was stiff and that could have killed her if the
vet hadn't come out. If it's a sheep now or a thing like that
you'd throw them into a trailer and bring them in.

These are sucklers out there. They're a mix of everything.
They're black Limousins. They'd have been mixed with a
Limousin and Friesian so they'd be good milkers. We have
focused on the Charolais so a lot of those white-looking cows
are Charolais. They're fine strong cows for this kind of terrain.
That red Whitehead is one of our oldest cows. The year my
father died she went down. She was actually down for eleven
days. The footing went from under her after calving. She had

a deficiency of something like calcium or she was a long time calving and she went weak in the back pins and wouldn't stand. We had guys helping us to lift her. I'd be drawing up bits of silage to her, buckets of nuts and stuff and she stood up and she reared the calf as well that year which was great. And this is now four years on and she has had nearly the best calf every year. It was a good decision to keep her.

It is very satisfying work when it's going good, especially at this time of year when all you have to do is come down and look at the animals but during the summer I came down and there was a cow with mastitis and a calf with maggots in his head from being skulled. My husband came down that night and he treated them. The calf just got the head washed out with a particular wash and he put tubes up the cow and milked her out. He had to do that daily. We're an hour-and-a-half away from here so that is the one drawback.

Now at the moment we're looking at the shed and I have the weanlings inside. I've fourteen weanlings in here. They're all Charolais weanling calves. There are four heifers here in the middle pen. They're very good heifers. We're going to fatten them up for about another month and we'll put them to the mart. They would be fairly valuable heifers now. If I wasn't going to Australia for Christmas we'd be keeping them until Eastertime but I have to sell off this year because I won't be around to be maintaining them myself.

We have the slatted shed here now over five years. We find it so good to put in the cattle for the winter because of our range of land. It's away easier to come down here and have everything housed inside in front of you. Over here then we have the bigger bullocks all being fed. We're actually using weanling crunch at the moment. It is Kerry Group food and we're delighted with it. They have an automatic feeder and they help themselves to it and they can manage away without us being here. They're fine. They seem to be happier than the cows. Some of these now would have been January calves, some March and some are even April calves. The smaller calves won't make half the value. You see they're away smaller because the cows went late and that's the thing that happens.

'I know there have to be regulations from the environmental point of view but there is a lot of red tape with farming today, a lot of book-work, and it can actually turn people off.'

We're in the low part of the farm here now. We're down below the road. It's very rough ground altogether. If the sheep came down here they wouldn't stop because it's not wired in for sheep. It is electric-fenced to hold the cattle. You have to have a special wiring for sheep to keep them contained. So they are up above the road here. We have about eighty lambs fattening now. They'll be sold to the factory or to the mart. What we have here out on the hill would be maybe 120 sheep because you'd have dry sheep up the hill. And we'd have about 150 then getting ready for the ram this year that we've kept from lambs ourselves. We have three rams that we're going to run with them. Sometimes we hold back a Scotch ram. We reduced our numbers and we started breeding with Texel and Suffolk ram to produce a lamb that fattens well and that we can finish well, ready for the factory. That's where we make our money and it's the kind of system that suits us. We have had special feeders brought in that we can fill a couple of times a week and it saves us coming down. They're kind of self-maintained once they're fed. It is the same with the calves. We have automatic feeders outside as well. They have to be filled up a couple of times a week and then they feed away themselves. So that makes it easy. We always have to look at ease of management because of the distance and the time it takes to get here.

You see a lot of different breeds of sheep here. Here now are our weaned lambs. These are male lambs. We have a mixture of crosses of Texel, Suffolk and Cheviot lambs. The Suffolks really do the best even though they are a soft lamb when they are born. The late lambing really helped. It's away easier to have them later so I think that's the way it's going to go from now on. We kind of just tried that out this year. We sell these to the factory as a group in November. Eighty of these lambs will go off together on the day. We usually have a customer base of twenty people, friends of ours who say, 'We'd like a lamb for Christmas,' and we'd fill that market as well. We're feeding them with nuts and some maize meal here at the moment. The price of feeding has gone up very much this year and I actually question whether it is even worth it.

A great friend of ours, Joe Tadhg, sheared the sheep with my husband one day. I was against the shearing from the point of view that they looked so lovely and fluffy before shearing but now I can see how they cleaned up well and they're building up lovely. This great autumn has been very helpful. There are no rams here now. The big sheep over there now is a wether. He's actually a castrated male lamb. You'd hear them refer to a two-year-old wether at the mart. That fellow there now was only castrated quite recently. He's still kind of running because he's a lad that escaped. Now if you were to kill him the meat would be very strong. It would have a very strong smell. I'd say if he got a bit of time to fatten up there'd be demand for a two-year-old wether in the factories. There are a lot of people that prefer wether to a yearling lamb. We find these lambs would be beautiful now. And anyone that we have sold them to is really looking for more.

We kill a beef roughly every year. We'd have a couple of lambs as well every year. It's absolutely fabulous. Would I have any compunction about looking into their eyes and feeding them and then killing them and eating them? I actually say to the children at the table, 'Don't talk about the food and where it comes from,' because I would stop eating. If you were to think about the process of how it got to the table you wouldn't even think of eating. We're fine fit-looking people and I think a lot of it is because we're eating our own food. We have no growth promoters. We have pure natural Kerry mountain sheep. If people weren't going to eat it there would be no sheep. I eat this myself and I have no problem in selling it on. We have no problems with traceability. This is pure mountain sheep and it's healthy.

Sometimes I ask myself what we are doing all this for. When things go wrong you can get right sick of it. Sometimes you'd see them bringing in regulations that don't make much sense and that are going to cost the farmer more. If they came down here and had to do it our way for a while they might think differently. I know there have to be regulations from the environmental point of view but there is a lot of red tape with farming today, a lot of book-work, and it can actually turn people off. In one of the studies that I did on work-life balance in farming they say that for the few hours you give doing books you'd make more on it than you would from doing the physical work. Maybe you're better paying someone to do the physical work. Still I think it is great for the mind, especially for somebody who is studying like me because it takes me away from the books. I have a lot of space and freedom.

I'm doing my masters in occupational psychology at

Leicester University now. I registered for second year in September and I have two more modules to do and I then have to do my dissertation. I will have to study 150 people working in industry and I begin my chartership before January 2008. I have just been passed to become a trainee psychologist with the British Psychological Society. I can do that part-time for the rest of my life but I will always run the farm as well.

Noreen Hanafin

Noreen Hanafin (41) lives with her husband in Puck Island, Lispole. She farms a large dairy herd, looks after their three children, works part-time with an optician and is an active member of her local community.

I was born and reared on a farm in Annascaul. There were just three girls in the family. We had no brother and my father worked us to the bone. We did every kind of work. That time it was all hard labour, whereas now they have a machine for everything. My father involved me in farming at an early age. I was born and reared with it. We had a small farm and my father was in receipt of the small farmers' dole. He had his own potatoes and vegetables. During the summer the three of us would spend weeks on the bog cutting turf with my father. All the turf was brought home and it did us for the whole winter. Times have changed very much. It was unheard of in those days to have a summer job. We had to help out on the farm and we daren't say we weren't going to do it and you daren't answer your parents back. You just had to get on with it. My mother and I would milk the cows but my father seldom milked. We milked with the hand buckets as there was no pipeline that time. We'd put the clusters on the cows and we'd have to empty the buckets. Indeed it was very strenuous work. My father would be looking after the sheep and the pigs. My two sisters always helped my father whereas I helped my mother. There was no machinery in those days. Most things were done by hand. My interest started there.

I went to a boarding school. My father sent my youngest sister and me to Coláiste Íde, an all-Irish boarding school in the west of Dingle. That detached us a bit from the farm but when we'd come home on our holidays there would be plenty work waiting for us. At boarding school we had a bit of a break from the farming until my Leaving Certificate. I was awfully sorry I didn't train to be a teacher then. My middle sister stayed at home but as it happened it was my youngest sister that got the farm. My father always had Friesian bulls on show. He would show them in Castleisland. So did my husband's father. Really that's where I got to know my husband first. Then I met him later at the Hillgrove in Dingle where we would go dancing. I was going out with him for about two or three years before we married. My children were all educated through Irish at primary and secondary level and both my husband and I are fluent Irish speakers.

I now live three miles from the place where I grew up. We built an extension onto my husband's parents' house. My husband inherited the farm from his father. It is mainly a dairy enterprise we have, consisting of eighty cows and just a few sheep. My husband really depends on me to help on the farm. We work very well together and that really is the making of a very good enterprise. Nowadays you have to keep making improvements and enlarging your farm if you want to stay in the business. Most of the money we make is ploughed back into the farm. When my husband got the farm there were only about twenty cows here and we have bought a lot of land and milk quota since. We have about 130 acres and we also take some land in grazing.

On a typical day my husband would be up about an hour or so before me. I take the kids to school – two trips at different times. I'd come home then and wash up after milking, power-hosing the parlour twice a day. There are strict guidelines to be adhered to in dairy farming. Hygiene is very important and your milking parlour can be inspected any time by Department officials. We milk together if needs be but I would have no problem milking on my own. Spring is our busiest time of the year as our cows are all spring calvers and therefore our routine changes dramatically. It is a twenty-four hour day and just total dedication. We made life easier for ourselves by installing a twelve-unit milking parlour. It can fit fourteen cows up a line now and we can milk eighty cows in an hour and a half. We sell most of our calves before six weeks, only keeping the Friesian heifer calves as replacements for our dairy herd. I manage the feeding of the calves in the springtime while my husband milks the cows.

It is difficult juggling farming with home life and children. After milking in the evening you'll have to come into the house and get a supper and the children have to be helped with their homework. In ways it is a good life but it is a hard life especially in the springtime. You have to forget about housework and just do the basics. I have three children who still need my individual attention. I have a nineteen-year-old son, a daughter who is fifteen and doing her Junior Cert and my youngest is twelve and in her final year in primary school. Any after-school activities for children in the evenings seem to revolve around cow time. Obviously non-farming people are not aware of our schedule.

You have to keep putting money into the farm – otherwise you won't have the returns from it. Every year there is something new to be invested in. Now you have to have a dairy hygiene certificate to supply milk to the co-op. Everywhere has to be spotlessly clean. Other requirements are

having wash-up troughs, a sink, a locked cabinet for all drugs, hot water and guards over all motors and machines. Long ago they hardly had a sink in the house, not to mind the milking parlour. At the moment a lot of farmers in my area are putting up slurry towers to accommodate all their slurry under EU rule. They cost between €30,000 and €40,000, depending on the size of your herd. They are also grant-aided.

At the moment dairy farming is the best that there is in farming. The price of milk is very good whereas if you were in sheep or suckler cows there is no way you could make a living solely from either of these. Only for all the money that's coming from Europe farming would be non-existent, especially for sheep and suckler farmers. In dairy farming you have a lot more expense because you have to keep upgrading your system and therefore investing a lot more money to make it profitable. You would want to be milking between eighty and a hundred cows to have a reasonable living out of it, whereas with a sheep or suckler farm you could work outside the farm. That is impossible with a dairy enterprise. Our milk is collected every three days by Kerry Group but you have to have a milk tank large enough to hold it for four days. The milk has to be of top quality, otherwise you will not get the top rate for it. It has to pass a lot of tests. One is the cell count which it has to be under 400, otherwise you will be fined so much a litre. There is also a quality test which is based mainly on hygiene. These regulations have put a lot of farmers out of business as they could not meet these requirements. If you can stick with it and keep investing and upgrading your farm, it will pay off eventually.

Teagasc would be our main advisory service and they call

every now and then. They have a lot of different views, some practical and some not. A lot of young fellows go to agricultural college for a year now, either to Pallaskenry or Clonakilty. I think it is a great experience for them and gives them a lot of different ideas and skills. I think the youngsters aren't interested in farming at all. They are just not prepared to put the work into it. The hours are long and with dairy farming you have to be there morning and evening to milk the cows. In recent years they have been enticed by the very high wages in the construction and other industries. We involved our children in farming at an early age. They don't seem to have much interest in it at the moment but hopefully that will change. My son does not work full-time on the farm. He works in construction but he helps out in the evenings with the milking and especially in the springtime when we are very busy. Sometimes my daughters help me with the feeding of the calves.

I have other interests besides farming which I find very relaxing after the strenuous farm work. I love gardening. I have my own vegetable plot where I grow peas, carrots, parsnips, potatoes and lots more besides. All are purely organic, free of chemicals, which is of utmost importance to me. We eat our own produce, including our own lamb, which is also purely organic. Everything that people are eating now is full of chemicals so that is mainly why I decided to start a vegetable garden. I think every farmer should have their own vegetable patch but of course it is not easy to get time for everything as the farm is already a very busy place. I'm also very interested in all kinds of arts and craftwork and using my creative skills. I have attended many arts and craft classes which are held in our local school every autumn. In the month of August we have an agricultural show in Dingle town and I exhibit a lot of stuff there – cooking, arts and crafts, vegetables and flower arrangements from my flower garden. My husband also shows Scotch Ram lambs.

I am also involved in a few committees. We have a children's band here in Lispole. They get together every Friday night. The children learn music and set dancing and they also take part in various events, for example, the local St Patrick's Day parade. I'm involved in the organising of the uniforms for the band. It's very time-consuming but I enjoy it. I was also involved with Lispole Community Games for many years. Within the last year-and-a-half I have gone back to work outside the home and farm. I was ten years out of the workforce. Initially I did a six week back-to-work course run by FÁS. It was an excellent course and it gave me the confidence and skills to return to work. After leaving school I went to the IT in Tralee for two years and did secretarial studies. At the moment I work part-time for an optician in Dingle. It is very enjoyable work and it gives me my own identity. I have my own PRSI whereas I cannot make payments in my own right from the farm.

'My husband really depends on me to help on the farm. We work very well together and that really is the making of a very good enterprise. Nowadays you have to keep making improvements and enlarging your farm if you want to stay in the business.'

I am also secretary here on the farm. I deal with most of the never-ending paper work that applies to farming. Paperwork is a major pressure for farmers. You cannot afford to make any mistakes with form-filling or with any other records for the farm as it could have serious financial implications. All farmers have a herd register, the 'blue book' as we call it, registering all movement on and off the farm in one side of it while the other side contains all the medical records of sick animals on the farm. This book has to be continuously updated as department officials can call unannounced at any time to check this book. Yet again the springtime is the busiest time as all the newborn calves have to be registered and a permit obtained for the movement of calves from farm to farm. Computers have made life easier. There are a lot of excellent farm packages available and you can register the newborn calves online, which is less time-consuming and very efficient with fewer errors being made. I am responsible for all this paperwork on our farm, which is done mainly at night after all the physical work is completed. Most farmers cannot afford to hire a secretary to do this work so it puts added pressure on the farming family with all the regulations and restrictions that are in place now. Of course we must not forget the farm accounts which have to be submitted before the end of October every year.

Farming can be very isolating, more so nowadays as there are very few full-time farmers left. Many are farming part-time, working outside the farm during the day. Years ago most farmers took their milk to the creamery. It was a great meeting place. Now the lorries collect the milk every three or four days from the farmyard. Many farmers would not meet a human being from one end of the week to the next. So it is very important that farming families have a social life outside the family farm. With a dairy farm it's impossible to take a weekend off or go on holiday as a family as the cows have to be milked morning and evening. The farm always comes first. Even if there is work to be done in the house it has to take a back seat. The only time we all can get a break is in January when the cows are not milking. You are very limited in your choice of holiday destination in January, especially if you are looking for a sun holiday.

I suppose farming is a satisfying life but it is a hard life. You have to be interested in it to enjoy it. It's a lovely environment to bring up children. They are in touch with nature and they develop a caring attitude towards animals. At least they are not hanging around towns and street corners getting into mischief. Religion means a lot to me. I couldn't survive without it. My mother was very religious and I picked that up. A lot of people don't make time for Mass now. My children are made go. The two girls are very religious really. It's different with the men. Well, they see things differently.

I hope my account of life as a farming wife will open up a debate about the value of women's unpaid work which has contributed in no small way to the wealth of this country. As I see it women are worse off since the introduction of PRSI for the self- employed. In many cases they cannot make payments in their own right. In any self-employed partnership the husband depends on the wife who, as I've already said, gets no remuneration and somehow when she reaches pension age she now becomes 'the dependent'. Not all women have the necessary skills to return to the workforce. The least the government could do for this category of women like me is to pay them a pension in their own right, not the dependent spouse allowance. Prior to 1988 both spouses had their individual pensions.

Catherine Lenihan

Catherine Griffin Lenihan (64) lives at Woodville, an impressive Georgian house bought by Arthur Lenihan's grandfather (also Arthur) after he came back from the gold rush in Klondyke. She farmed in Gortatlea near Castleisland for most of her married life with her husband Arthur and their daughters. They retired from full-time farming in 2000.

I was born in St Catherine's Hospital in Tralee in 1943 and grew up about a mile-and-a-half from Castleisland. I was the eldest of four children, two boys and two girls. We were always farming. We had two aunts in the house who weren't married and I can remember my aunt driving us to school on a donkey and cart. We progressed to bicycles then. We cycled to secondary school. The roads were much safer then for cycling. There was no problem at all and we only had a mile-and-a-half to travel. We could have walked it and it was easier to walk. We'd have gone alone. Well you wouldn't go alone nowadays. The national school I attended in Castleisland was about a mile-and-a-half from home. All my teachers were nuns and they gave great attention to discipline in those days. There was a daily roll-call of all the pupils and generally no excuse would be taken for not having lessons done. The Irish language was taken very seriously. I learned History and Geography through Irish. In sixth class we did the Primary Certificate. A nun would supervise the playground while she was saying her prayers on a big rosary beads that hung from her habit. We used to take five shillings to school for dancing lessons and two shillings and sixpence (half a crown) for turf to keep the classroom heated in winter. We would be allowed up in pairs to warm our hands at the fire. We would bring a bottle of milk to school and place it close to the fire to take the chill out of it. Hygiene was practically non-existent. The toilet consisted of a wooden board with a circular hole in the centre and a stream running independently underneath. There was no toilet paper and no soap or towels.

I didn't have to do an awful lot of work outside but my mother was a great hand-milker. I never milked. I tried all right but I was never able to. She used to console me and she'd say that it was from years of practice that she got to be so good at it. I would often take the bucket of milk and empty it into the tank. There used to be gauze on top of the tank to strain the milk. My father would then take the tanks to the creamery either with a donkey and cart or a pony and cart. Later on then we got a milking machine but the milk still had to be drawn sometimes and the tanks had to be filled. We never made butter. My brother now farms the home farm where we all grew up. My other brother has his own farm. A lot of work had to be done to update it. There was a pencil quarry on the farm and they were able to use the pencil in the making of a new roadway at the entrance to the farm.

We had an old thatched house at home and I can remember the huge open fire with the crane and the griddle and pots and the black kettle that used to hang on it. My aunt would make lovely white soda bread. I think she had some art in the kneading of it which I was never able to acquire – like the hand-milking. We all helped out with the saving of the hay. My father cut it with the horse and mowing bar and then it was made into rows and sometimes if it wasn't fit we'd make small cocks. Then it would be made into wynds and tied with a twine. We wound the súgán too and used it sometimes instead of twine. The hay was brought home with a pony and a haycart. You'd wind it up with a handle. It would then be piked into the hayshed. I remember helping to trample the hay in the shed in order to level it.

I didn't ever work in the bog. The men worked in the bog and the women got the meals. They boiled the kettle on an open fire in the bog. A friend of ours had a fire and he would let them boil the kettle on it. Then the turf was cut with a sleán. When it was fit it would be footed and then stooked and then after a while it would be drawn out and made into a reek. When it was ready it was brought home by horse and cart. There would be another reek made of it at home and it would be covered with thatch. When we progressed to hiring a lorry for bringing home the turf it was a special treat to be taken for a drive to and from the bog.

We had our own corn as well. My father always cut corn. He would have to get the reaper and binder for the corn but he would cut the headlands himself with a scythe. It was brought home for thrashing then of course. There would be an awful crowd in the haggard on the day of the threshing and they all had their own jobs. They would help each other out. They used to call it comharing. We'd be comharing with the neighbours.

When I was growing up we kept pigs at home. My mother had the job of minding the sow when they'd be having banbhs and I often stayed up at night with her and you'd have to be very careful in case the sow would lie on them. My father always killed a few pigs in the year. We would salt them ourselves. It was customary when we'd kill the pig to give some pork steak and puddings to the neighbours and they in

turn would give it to you when they'd kill a pig. They made the puddings too. I can remember puddings being made but how it was done I'm not too sure. I remember the finished product and taking them to the neighbours. There was great sharing with neighbours in those days.

'My an aunt would make lovely white soda bread. I think she had some art in the kneading of it which I was never able to acquire – like the hand-milking.'

My father made a lot of friends in Castleisland on his way home from the creamery with the horse and cart. At the creamery the milk had to be separated and he would bring home the separated milk. He would have to travel through the town on his way home and there would be women waiting for him at different points and he'd give them separated milk for making bread. We set potatoes too of course and my father would give a couple of drills to neighbours who wouldn't have land. One such neighbour was Peg Brosnan who was living back the road. She died last week and at the funeral we were just reminiscing about that. She used to plant the potatoes and dig them. There's a special way of cutting the seed potatoes and not everybody could do it but my neighbour Mary Quilter had the knack. There's nobody around here as far as I know who would set their own vegetables now and it's a pity really, isn't it? It's all vegetables from the supermarkets now.

I did my Leaving Cert in 1961 and then I worked as a telephonist in the post office for eight or nine years. I met my husband in Castleisland at a dance. The dances were very good. We were very lucky to have the dances in comparison with nowadays. After working a number of years in the post office I married Arthur, who lived only a short distance from my own home. As well as farming at home Arthur continued the tradition of selling milk in Castleisland. I had to get used to the political scene then as Arthur was a county councillor, as were his father and grandfather before him. Arthur's grandfather, Arthur Lenihan, emigrated to America in 1880 and when gold was found in the Klondyke Valley in Yukon, Canada he travelled up there and ran a trading post. He operated a little haulage business. In 1904 he sold his stake and returned to Ireland and with the money he made bought a farm at Ballinvariscal. He and his brother Jack married two sisters and they all lived there. In 1919 Woodville came on the market with ten acres. Arthur bought the house and ten acres and he moved there with his wife. He divided the farm between himself and his brother. Well that's the Georgian house we live in now and it is a couple of hundred years old. A house this size would have had a few servants in the olden days. Arthur's wife was a great artist and she was good at gardening. That's not continued now.

My mother-in-law, with whom I had a great relationship, helped with the cows and with the rearing of our five girls. She had her own section of the house. She liked to have her own quarters but she was a marvellous woman. She helped out with the milking and feeding calves. I wasn't accustomed to milking parlours and she explained the mechanism to me. I didn't keep hens since I got married here but we had hens at home in my parents' place. We kept hens and ducks and a couple of turkeys. My mother-in-law kept them too but she had to give it up because the fox would carry off every one of them.

'There would be an awful crowd in the haggard. on the day of the threshing. and they all had their own jobs. they would help each other out. They used to call it "comharing."'

There was a tradition here of selling liquid milk. Charlie Lenihan had a butcher's shop in Castleisland and he used to sell milk there. He started it and then my husband continued it. We would get up at about six o'clock in the morning and the milk had to be got ready for Castleisland. We had about four ten-gallon tanks. They had to be cooled with an immersion cooler and then my husband would put them into the van and take them to Castleisland. My mother-in-law and I would feed the calves. We had a farm labourer as well. There was plenty of work for everybody.

Farm labourers were treated very well on the whole and they often happened to be relatives of the farmers but you would hear the odd story about those who were not treated well. Having said that, they were never short of milk for their families as the farmers generally would give them big bottles of milk going home in the evenings after their day's work. You would hear stories too about the workmen who had to sleep in outhouses but I never knew of any. Nowadays the farm labourer has his own transport and usually travels to work by car. The farmer has to pay a social insurance stamp for his workman so that if he is ill he can claim benefits. There were no such benefits in earlier days.

When we were dairying we had to work from morning until night. It was a long day starting at six and it could go on and on. The cows mightn't be finished until seven or eight o'clock in the evening. I never drove the tractor but my children did. My two elder girls were very small when they were able to drive. My father-in-law grew vegetables. I remember there were potatoes planted when I came. They planted a small quantity for some years but we have not planted any in recent years. There was a big orchard there where the new milking parlour is now. I'm here thirty-five years and my girls have all grown up. They have got on very well and Arthur and I are very proud of them. We're retired from farming now. At the moment we have the farm leased until 2010.

Before we leased the farm we always cut turf. It's all

machine-cut now and they sell it by the row. They brought home some of it here yesterday. We only got five rows. That's all we wanted because we had a good bit left over since last year. We heat only the kitchen with the turf. We have hot water out of the range. It's just the kitchen area but we put a fire in the sitting-room in the winter and it serves a few radiators upstairs. We have no central heating, just the few radiators off the fire.

Since we retired from farming we don't even keep a sheepdog around the place. We had greyhounds. My husband was very interested in greyhounds at one stage but that seems to have fizzled out. We had one up to a few years ago but he was only a pet. He'd sleep inside at night. He had to be put down for a finish when he got very sick. So that's why I didn't want another one. I'd hate to have to put them down. We nearly got out of cats completely at one stage. We've six or seven at the moment. I find there is great security in them for the vermin as long as they're kept outside. They had an awful habit of coming in at one stage. Farmers don't usually like to have the animals anywhere inside. I feed them outside. I look after them a couple of times a day. We neutered a couple of cats here but we didn't ever neuter a dog.

With all the modern amenities farming has got easier but the weather is a big factor. In recent years modern machinery has made saving hay and making silage a lot easier. It is physically easier anyway. There was no such thing as farm relief in earlier days. It was a full-time job seven days a week. Farm relief gave people a better chance of taking time out. With the Farm Relief Scheme there are a lot more people available and they have a lot of foreign nationals on their books. Well, in our immediate area here now I don't think there are any but I heard that in the relief office in Castleisland they are employing them. The women have made a big impact on modern farming and very often it's the women do the accounts as well. It's a job in itself now. There's more equality now definitely.

'My mother-in law, with whom I had a great relationship, helped with the cows and with the rearing of our five girls. She had her own section of the house. She liked to have her own quarters but she was a marvellous woman. She helped out with the milking and feeding calves.'

The environment is a very big issue now. Anybody involved in the REPS scheme has to keep the farm up to a certain standard. We weren't in it ourselves. You can't have pollution. You have to have plenty of storage tanks. All those schemes have made people cop on to themselves. They can't just have the place any old way. They have to have hedges and everything right and sheds have to be properly painted. They

get some money but they then have to keep a certain number of cattle per acre.

Social isolation is talked about in farming but it's a woman's own fault now if she hasn't social contact because the ICA is everywhere and there are a lot of farming women in it. I must say I didn't have much social contact really except for the few neighbours and my friends. Nowadays there are more women in the ICA than there would have been in my time.

'I used to knit at one time ... I hadn't time when I got married but I knitted before I got married. I knitted a good few Aran sweaters ... I found it sort of relaxing.'

As for interests or hobbies outside the home I like to go for a walk and I would read a bit but while farming full-time and rearing five children we were always very busy. I didn't have much free time. I read nothing very deep now, preferably something easy. Farming life was the only life I knew. You have freedom in one sense and plenty of fresh air. I couldn't ever imagine myself living happily in a town. I like the contact with animals, especially feeding calves. Women are more equal now and they are having fewer children and consequently they have more time. We spent an awful lot of time rearing the children. I used to knit at one time. We learned it in school in those days. They don't teach it at all now. Well, at school we would have knitted only caps and scarves. We learned how to turn the heel of a sock. I hadn't time when I got married but I knitted before I got married. I knitted a good few Aran sweaters just for my own family and I liked knitting. I found it sort of relaxing. My two older girls learned how to knit at school but they never knitted anything afterwards. It was only the two older ones and I think they had stopped teaching it after that.

Some old customs have died out. I heard of piseogs when I was growing up. They would put eggs into wynds of hay so that the hay would come to no good. The whole idea was to damage the person. They would get the benefit then so that their crop would be better. I don't think it happened very often or was it just farmers that would do it? It was a form of putting a curse on somebody I think. Well that's died out now a long time, a couple of generations, and it's no loss either.

There have been a lot of changes in recent years. Religion and faith don't play as big a role among farming women today but you still have prayer meetings. They have them in Castleisland and Scartaglen. People would meet at them. It's hard to generalise. You still have people who are genuinely religious but the influence of the Church is waning. Marriages among the farming community would tend to be stable compared to society as a whole. That would be my impression.

'I heard of piseogs when
I was growing up. They would
put eggs into wynds of hay
so that the hay would come
    to no good. The whole idea
was to damage the person.'

Mary
Lenihan

Mary Lenihan (43) farms in Toureen, Ballymacelligot with her husband John. Apart from the demands of her dairy herd she is a dedicated animal-lover and plays host to a great variety of rabbits, goats, dogs, cats, ducks, hens, bantams and peacocks.

I met my husband John through running. We both run. He would come into the shop where I worked and he'd take me out dancing. It was about five years after that that we married. It took us a long time! John's people owned this farm and I married in here. His family got to know me well because I would come up here on my days off and help out. Sometimes I would clean out the cowhouses. To come out here to a farm was an awful adjustment. It took me months to settle in after getting married. I didn't come from a farming background and hadn't much contact with animals when I was growing up. We had a cat and a dog at home but that was it. I grew up in the town of Castleisland which had bright lights, and then we got married in October which meant I was straight into darkness. All I had been used to was town traffic. It took me months to get to sleep here with the dogs barking. I was always on edge that there was something strange happening.

Before I married I worked with J. P. Griffin & Sons newsagents in Castleisland and I still work there part-time. I have been working there for twenty-five years. It was the only job I ever applied for in my life. I love working there but it is part-time now. I found that juggling work and farm life was getting more and more difficult. I was working until five or six in the evening and then coming home to work on the farm and I was not able to cope. I loved it so much I didn't want to give up work altogether and seriously with farming today you need a job with it. So John suggested part-time work. Now I'm usually home by 1.30 pm and then I fall into my farm work which I love. I have become a real farmer now. I wouldn't go back to a town. It's just the noise and the cars. I had to stay at my home one time and I could hear the noise of cars and I thought it was so completely different. I couldn't get over it. There were no dogs barking and there was constant light coming in the windows. Now when I wake up in the morning we have hens and ducks and cocks and they're crowing. I have two peacocks and the very minute the light is dawning they start. In the springtime they could start about five o'clock.

The peahen hasn't laid yet. I got the two of them as a present and the fox killed her mate so I scouted around and I got another one but she doesn't seem to take to him. I didn't know anything about peacocks and I looked it up and found that they only mate once. I have them confined again now because of the fox. There are a lot of woodlands here and you can actually smell the foxes in the yard sometimes. That's why we always let out a dog at night. Sometimes they can fool the dogs. I've seen it happen myself where they'd come in the back and take the dogs away and then another fox would come through on the other side. I let out the fowl now but they go into bed at a certain time.

I have Rhode Island hens and I hatch my own eggs. I have lovely Peking Bantam cocks with fur on their legs. I have no hens in those. They have to be kept inside in case of the fox. They are very rare and they would be too precious. Once it starts to get dusk I make sure everything has gone in. I had a lot of hens but ten would be the outside now. I don't sell the eggs because sometimes they hatch on the eggs themselves so

I get more chickens. I break some of the eggs into the milk and give them to the dogs to make a lovely shine on their coats.

The dogs are pampered. Sometimes you'd have nothing and all of a sudden all the hens are laying and then you're trying to find houses to put them into. I wouldn't mind if all the chickens lived. No matter how much you try some of them will die and some will live. I had thirteen this year and we had a bad storm there a couple of months ago. There was thunder and lightening and when I went out all I had left was nine. They got a fright and died of shock but they were very small, only a couple of days old. I raised those nine chickens this year. A lot of the hens are old and sometimes they wouldn't lay at all. I'd never just twist the neck off them and eat them when they get old. I let them die peacefully. I'd eat the eggs all right. I'm vegetarian but I wasn't brought up as one. We'd eat meat at home but when I saw my first calf being born I couldn't after that. My husband would eat meat.

I have ten dogs now. Some of them were strays and a lot of them had been dropped off. We picked up two recently at a quarry. A lot of people don't want their dogs. I try to find new homes for them but what happens is I get attached to them. They start to mingle and it's really hard then. If you give them to somebody else would they have the same care? You can see it in their eyes if they have been neglected and then they're so happy with the rest of the dogs. I've been getting stale bread from people and I buy dog food and dog biscuits for them. Since I have such a lot of dogs I have to neuter them.

I have only three cats at the moment. I had a lot but they died of old age. I'm down to three kittens that I got from my mother-in-law weeks ago. Well, hopefully they'll keep the

mice at bay. I have ten rabbits. I have six indoors at the moment and I have four in a shed to be put out next spring. I always had a fascination with rabbits. I longed for a rabbit and then I felt that when we were out working he wouldn't have enough companionship so I got another one and it went from there. Then I saw two more and I ended up with ten of them. There are some lovely breeds there. I have three Australian Reds and they're gorgeous altogether. They're the big ones. They're supposed to grow about two feet long, about the size of a small Jack Russell. I have three Lion Heads as well and they're all different colours. The Lion Head is the one with the big hairy mane. Out in the shed I have two ordinary ones. Most of them are pure breeds. I buy them and don't breed them at all. My husband doesn't mind the animals inside and outside. He knows I look after them well. They get their injections every year. I get up in the morning and feed them and clean them out. He knows I love animals. I don't think I could survive up here if I didn't. We don't have children.

I have eight goats. Two of them are real pets altogether. They go for a run with us. We actually found those two. About two years ago John was going counting cattle when he found this little kid and we called her Buttercup. She was only about a day or two old but her neck was cut and she was ready to die. Maybe foxes or mink attacked them and the mother ran off. John brought her home so that she would not die in the field where there were crows on the branches of the trees overhead just waiting for her to die. We took her to the vet and she was so unrecognisable you wouldn't know what animal she was. He injected her and told us she had a murmur in the heart and other complications. I bought a bag of 'Frisky' and

had to feed her twice during the day and twice at night. Her neck was so mangled you had to prop her head up on the corner of the box to feed her as she had no strength to move her head or body. Once she drank her bottle you would have to wait until she fell asleep to adjust her into her box. She would choke if her head was left propped on the corner of the box. Some nights I would be up for an hour or more with her at feeding time. She would not go to sleep straight away. I spent months doing that. We reared her upstairs in what we call John's computer room because that room has heat. She had to learn to stand and walk. It was nearly six months before we could let her outside with the other animals. She is good now but we still have to watch her tightly. Our vet is brilliant. I come down to him with the queerest of things. He takes no notice. I've gone with a cockerel that lost its feathers and I had to give it ten tablets, one a day, to get back the feathers.

I don't milk any of the eight goats. They're all pets. One had triplets and the other one had twins so they all added up. I got the males neutered and I kept them as well. They're all outside in the paddock there. We have one with the cows. He stays with the cows and doesn't ever seem to mix with the goats. The mother goat had triplets and she was mad about two of them but she kept shooing this fellow away so I had to bottle-rear him. When he grew up he didn't want to mix with the goats but preferred to be with the calves and when they grew into cows he stayed with them.

I get up in the morning and milk with John at the busy milking time. I have the best of both worlds. This time of the year I go to work at half-past eight so I don't have to do the milking but in the springtime I'd be up around six o'clock. I like someone to be there when I'm working the milking machine because I have been kicked. I'd bring in the cows and if there's someone with me I'd put the clusters on them. I wouldn't trust them on my own even though I'm here twelve years. I should be used to it but when they get so big I just don't trust them. You can never trust a cow really.

'Her neck was cut and she was ready to die. John brought her home so that she would not die in the field where there were crows on the branches of the trees overhead just waiting for her to die. We reared her upstairs in what we call John's computer room because that room has heat. She had to learn to stand and walk.'

When it comes to cows I don't have as much affection for them but when they are calves I do. I'm up in the morning with John feeding them. John doesn't tell me when he's selling them sometimes. We bucket-feed them in the spring. I'd name them all and John would say which cow's milk belongs to which calf. When you name them they're kind of personal. Once they grow up it doesn't matter what names they have. You still have new ones to replace them with. We didn't get to the pigs yet. If we went into pigs they'd be called Babe and I think it would kill me!

John had to do a farm-management course to take over the

farm here. We weren't married when he did that course. I kind of fell in with it and that's it. Between dry cows and milking cows we have about seventy-two. The milk is not collected from here. There's no way they'd come up our road so we have to take it all the way down to the creamery. We have a big bulk tank and it goes down every three days. When John milks I collect some for my dogs before we put it into the tank. He doesn't mind. A good lot of milk goes on them. John has a part-time job as well because the farm wouldn't keep us. We would be considered small. We have only twenty-four milking cows so you'd need another job just to keep going. He works on a scheme called Tuatha Chiarraí from nine until four, nineteen hours a week and the rest is farming. I don't drive even though I am nearly seven miles from town but at one time I actually ran to work. I would get up in the morning to milk the cows with John and once I had my jobs done I'd put on my running gear, a rucksack on my back to carry my clothes for work, and then I'd run into town. Now we both start at almost the same time in the morning so I don't run into work any more.

We cut our own hay and silage every year. We draw bales of hay. The cows are fed hay and silage and we give them ration as well. We have to buy ration at different times of the year. Mostly it would be the dairy nuts. I actually put in the ration and bring in the cows for John if he's very late coming home. The weather plays a big part in saving the hay and the silage. This year was very bad but we have great friends and neighbours, a great bunch of people. We just tell them we are starting it and they'd all come over. They'd draw in the bales with us. Most of them wouldn't even be farmers. They'd be

actually running partners with John. There is a great community spirit here. If they knew that you were stuck and the weather was bad they would come.

We farm nearly all the land, cutting off some of it for hay and silage. We strip-feed the fields. The rules in farming today are desperate. You'd hear John's dad talking about the time he was farming. There are so many different rules coming in. Some of them are good but many of them don't work everywhere. It is really hard to agree with the tagging. They have to do it, I suppose, but I'd hope there would be some other way of doing it than tagging them. Sometimes you'd see animals there and the tag has gone off their ear and it's sore.

We make joint decisions. Fair play to John he would let me have my say in what's going on. There is equality. I mean you have to in a marriage. You mightn't agree all the time but you still have to let the other person have their say. John does the accounts on his computer and he is better with the money. If I see a thing and my animals need it I'll buy it but he'd be more practical and you have to be. I can't use the computer. I never learned, can't even put it on. I'd be afraid to break it so I just don't touch these things. John did a course for a couple of weeks inside in Tralee on how to use the computer. That would be a big break from the time when his father was a farmer. We have an accountant to look over our books and take all of what we have into account. We'd do that once a year. We don't actually have telephone poles coming to the house. There was a box at the corner of the house like a transmitter. About two years ago they updated it and we got the internet in but I don't think we have broadband yet.

This is an old house. I think John's grandmother was in her

'I suppose I could get somebody to feed them and clean out from there but I feel they couldn't look after them because the animals all have their own little quirky ways.'

teens or twenties when this house was built. It goes back over a hundred years. When we got married John's ninety-nine-year-old grandmother who was living here got sick and went into hospital and she stayed there until her death at a hundred and one. She was a great age. When we moved in there was no one here. We had a lot of repairs to do when we came. We took off all the dry lining and we plastered the walls and painted them. We had built-in presses which was the wrong thing to do because it's an old stone house. The dampness would come through. We had to take the presses off the walls again. They are really meant to be free standing here. I didn't realise it at the time. That was a big expense but you learn by your mistakes, don't you? It has three bedrooms and we added on the conservatory. When you come in the back door you can throw your wellingtons and the whole lot out there.

Before I came to the farm I would go to the bog every summer with my mother and father and my sister to my father's uncle's place in Gleanntawn and we'd foot and stack our turf and bring it home. We have our own bog here now and we save our own turf. We haven't cut it in a couple of years because the machine cuts it for us. They cut it in lines, hoppers they call them. Then we just turn the sods. I go up

and turn it, which is kind of hard because I'm left-handed. Usually they stay out of my way when I'm turning it with the pike. I'll go up there and foot it and stack it and bring it home. The house is heated by our own turf. We don't have oil at all. I threw out the range. I'm not a great cook so I found it was wasting a lot. I put in a little stove and we heat ten radiators off that. It does the whole house. We are really self-sufficient in fuel and milk but we buy vegetables.

'A lot of people don't want their dogs. I try to find new homes for them but what happens is I get attached to them ... you can see it in their eyes if they have been neglected and then they're so happy with the rest of the dogs.'

I've always wanted to set a garden but I don't know if I would be good at it. My father always had his own garden. He grew potatoes, cabbage and onions and I'm sorry I didn't learn. You go through life and there are things you should have learnt. John wouldn't mind but I'd buy organic vegetables myself. They are a lot more expensive but still I think you are kind of helping, aren't you? It's kind of the way to go. Some day I'll get to setting things as well. The goats would come in and eat them but if I could keep them off it I'd be fine. I would like to be self-sufficient but we're not that way yet. I'm not a great eater. I'd probably have porridge in the morning and if I could go for the rest of the day on cups of tea I'd be fine. I really have to eat to keep running so I'll have apples and I'd have beans on toast but I'm not a great lover of cheese.

I love my fashions and on the occasions that I dress up I get my hair done and I have the high boots and the knee-high socks and the whole lot. My style icons would be Sienna Miller, Kate Moss and Victoria Beckham. I took up pilates in Tralee for six weeks. It's about posture mainly and I do that just to get flexible. I love running and I'd still run. I ran at competitive level but I don't any more. John is in the Ríocht club and I joined it before I got married. John is into big-time climbing. He actually holds the record for running on Carrantuohill, up and down in seventy-one minutes. That was twenty or twenty-one years ago and his record has not been beaten. He trains around here. On Tuesday nights a group of them meet and they all go training together. He went to England this year. A group of about fifteen of them climbed Scafell Pike and then they went from that to Snowden. That's his social life. My social life would be around sporting activities too and when I come home I stay here. I love it. A lot of people would just pop up. I know it's a long way up. They leave their car at the end of the road and walk up. Christmas is a good time. We have a night when all of us gather here. We really wouldn't have dinner parties. I don't drink. Usually we just sit down and have a laugh and a joke together.

We don't go away on holidays together. We both can't go.

One of us would have to stay. I have too many animals and I can't go away so John would go. I suppose I could get somebody to feed them and clean out from them but I feel they couldn't look after them because the animals all have their own little quirky ways. I suppose in a way they tie me down but the reward is when I look in their eyes and see that they're so happy. They want to come up in my lap. I couldn't go away from that, honestly. I would be worrying about them. Even at night now I have everything in and I'm checking before I go to bed. Is everything all right and is everything in its place?

I am a half-twin. My sister Catherine lives in Castleisland with her husband Humphrey. Would Catherine live in Toureen? No! She is not the one to ring if you have a cow calving but if you say that you want to paint a room or two, Catherine, Humphrey and Mom are up to you straight away. They even bring their own brushes with them as long as I supply the paint! Catherine and I are so different, yet we are alike in many ways. We are like two sides of a coin. She owns a dog. That's it! I don't think my mother has ever seen so many rabbits, maybe in a pet shop but not in a house.

My animals are my pride and joy. The affection you get back from them is something else. When I get up in the morning now and I have my cereal they pop out from underneath their cages. Then they start eating because I have started. I just like simple pleasures. As long as none of them dies I'm happy. Only for the support from John and both our families and friends, my bosses and all the animals I would not survive up here really. They have all played a part in defining who I am today.

'Our vet is brilliant. I come
down to him with the
queerest of things. He takes
no notice. I've gone with a
cockerel that lost its feathers
and I had to give it ten tablets,
one a day, to get back the
feathers.'

Breda Lynch

Breda Lynch (47) is a sheep farmer in Coorleigh, Bonane. She has been awarded the title of All-Ireland Sheep-Shearing Champion on six occasions and still takes part in competitions, sometimes against her two sons. She loves her sheep and cattle and her beloved hills, despite the difficulties of hill farming and the lack of financial rewards. She has a fierce interest in the precious nature of the land in all its cruelties and hardships.

I grew up in Coomhola near Bantry about nine miles across the hill from this farm but if I went around by the road it would be twenty-two miles. I still call it home. I still shout for Cork but once Cork is losing the football or hurling I'll shout for Kerry. There's big tension in this house when Cork and Kerry are playing in a final. I had to do a lot of farmwork when I was a child. I had two sisters and one brother. My eldest sister gave Dad a great hand farming but my brother and my other sister never took to the farming. I was the youngest of the family and I think I was cut out for farming from day one. Depending on what time of the year it would be you'd have to do work before you went to school. In the springtime you'd have to check the sheep before you'd go for fear there'd be young lambs there and if there was a weak lamb you'd be running to the kitchen with him and putting him near the fire to help him survive.

We had cattle as well. We had a few cows and we were going to the creamery when I was very young. There were only eleven cows there and they were milked by hand. I was milking as soon as I was able to pull the teat and I was only eleven years old when I started shearing the sheep with the hand-shears. My father never saw me shearing with the electric shears because he died suddenly of a heart attack when I was just twenty. It was an awful blow to me. Denis Harrington, my neighbour, had sheep and he wanted me to go shearing with him. He took away my hand-shears and gave me his shears for the price of my own. It was easy to cut the sheep with the machine if I wasn't holding them in the right position. There's a lot in machine shearing. There's fierce control. You've only your legs and one hand to control the movements. It was the first bit of money I made. Well that time I suppose I'd do nearly the hundred in a day. I was about twenty then. The best record I did was 248 in one day. You'd be talking about one minute thirty seconds per sheep. In these competitions you normally get two minutes to shear one sheep and time was never my issue. I'd always be out in the two minutes anyway so I'd be getting full marks. I was recently All-Ireland Sheep Shearing Champion. I won three years now in succession. Then this year I got sixth place in the Juniors National and it was a fierce achievement to get in against the men. I was shearing against my own son. I put him out of it and he put me out of another competition.

I have won the All-Ireland six times. I retired in 1985 when I had my child. I gave my time then to my child and I decided that I wouldn't do any more competition shearing. I was on top and I'd give someone else a chance – give the youth more rope. You see a lot of old shearers there every year. They're winning and they're giving no chance to the younger shearers. You'd get sick of going to the competitions with the same people winning every year. I came back three years ago and it was my son who introduced me back to it because he was following the shearing as well. And he'd say, 'Mom, if you were there you'd have won it.' I went to support him and I ended up shearing on the day. The competition was held in Pearse Stadium in Galway. I made my comeback. It was a mighty achievement. I can thank my son. There's no high like it. It's unreal. I've three or four days off in the year and that's to go to competition shearing. That's my social life. I'm not interested in getting out of my wellies and putting on the stilettos or shopping for style. I hate that with a passion. I never used make-up or lipstick or nail-varnish. I'd hate it. Aren't you only covering reality? I think so.

There are no two days the same when you are stuck with farming. You get up in the morning and there would be always something to do. My sheep are the biggest enterprise I have. The springtime is the busiest time of the year because you're watching them lambing. The weather has an awful lot to do with it of course. We lamb them outside. We don't stay up through the night now. Going through them by night I'd say we were only disturbing them. Foxes are a nuisance. They are a plague, a scald. We dazzle them by night and shoot them. They'd have us plagued only for the control we're putting on them and the time and the effort. Well we use a light. They're on open ground. The idea of the light is that you'd pick them up in the distance with their eyes. The fox's eye glows more than a sheep's eye but you could mistakenly shoot a dog and you'd always have to be cautious. You make sure your background is safe. I don't own a gun now. I had a licence for my father's gun for a few years but I left it back to the home place because it belonged to my grandfather and it's more of an antique now. I have no gun licence but my partner has a shotgun. My son has a shotgun as well as a rifle and he goes

'The best record I did was 248 in
one day. You'd be talking about
one minute thirty seconds per sheep...
I was recently All-Ireland Sheep
Shearing Champion. I won
three years now in succession.'

after the foxes a bit but he's involved too in clay pigeon shooting.

Well I have different breeds of sheep here but my main breed would be Scotch. You know I have a beggarman's bag (a mixed bag). I have a bit of Mayo and Swaledale for the higher part of the mountain. They'd be a great hardy breed of sheep. There are different types of Scotch. The Dingle Scotch now is a good ram. We go back to Dingle for the ram every year and buy a few rams at the mart. We'd have a great day in Dingle. We'd spend the whole day out. We'd make a day of it. That would be an annual outing. I go to Kenmare mart now and I could go to Skibbereen. I'd say I'm a dying tradition. Looking around me there isn't another woman doing what I'm doing in the locality. It's a part-time involvement for some of them but I'm full-time. I've no other job only farming.

I have cattle as well. I have seven pure-bred Shorthorn cows. I had pure-breds bar one when brucellosis hit us. They took away a beautiful heifer first and then three the next time. It was Christmas 1996 and I'll never forget it. It was like my family was going down the road in a hearse when the cattle went. I fought with the department. I was entitled to three tests and if I had a clear test in the third one I'd get more tests. If they stayed right I was entitled to keep my cattle until they'd go down. They tried depopulating them several times but I wouldn't let them go. I love my animals. So they came right for me and I was so happy. I'm still happy to see them there. Nine was the most I had in cows and I'd have the few heifer replacements and the few calves. The time doesn't go into them like sheep. There's way more work in sheep with dipping, dosing, shearing, marking and checking. They're a

'Well I have different breeds of
sheep here but my main breed would
be Scotch. You know I have a
beggarman's bag (a mixed bag). I
have a bit of Mayo and Swaledale
for the higher part of the mountain.'

full-time job. There isn't that much money out of them. And yet we pay such a high price for our lamb. It's ridiculous. The time and money that goes into them and you're not rewarded. You have no choice. What choice have we here in the hills? We haven't the land to go into grain. So you're married to the sheep here. It isn't suitable for cattle and my seven cows don't have the best of time. It's the summer on the hill for them. They never get into the fields because I give them silage for the winter. I close off the fields for eight weeks, weather permitting. My partner cuts the hay and I'll toss it out with the tractor and row it in for the baler. We'd have about a hundred bales and that's feeding for the cows for the winter.

'I've three or four days off in the year and that's to go competition shearing. That's my social life.'

I drive a tractor myself. It is very high hilly ground but you must do it. I got turned once and it nearly got me but my time wasn't up, I guess. We had only a two-wheel drive tractor at the time. I came down on the top of the height and I hit the grass and she took off and she got turned. Three-and-a-half times she turned but I was lucky – she threw me on the first turn. I came out the roof and she stayed rolling down. It was a fierce fright to get but thank God I'm alive to tell the story. Well, I never went into a field since with that tractor. I lost confidence altogether. We got a four-wheel drive tractor and I built up confidence with that. It's way safer. The two-wheel

drives are a nightmare on high ground. They're not suitable for it. I think the quad really is the best invention ever. They can be dangerous, there's no doubt, but they are a gift. I have one with a little trailer and we spread the manure with it. It is fierce handy if you go away wiring.

I enjoy the life. I know no different I suppose. I like working on my own. I go out there and tear away into something on my own, happy out. It is unreal to go out there in the night. You'd hear the fox barking and the deer whistling. Sure it's heaven. I don't watch television. I don't bother with it. The television is a joke. There's only violence on the television. Every time you turn it on sure it's only shooting or stabbing or fighting. There are no programmes like long ago. They used to have the programme with the dog Lassie. The only thing I watch of the soaps now would be *Home and Away* and I listen to Kerry radio. This is my world and it's small. I love farming. I wouldn't be at it only for I love it. You are your own boss more or less. There's no money being made. Sure what else could I go at? That's all I know. I was very young when I started to help my father at home. I left school when I was thirteen years. Well, I left because my father, Lord have mercy on him, he's dead now, his sight failed and he couldn't follow the sheep. If he went to the hill he couldn't even see the dog gathering the sheep. He was very upset about selling the sheep. I made him a promise. I said, 'Dad you don't have to sell the sheep. I'm big enough now and I'll see after the sheep.' That was fine. We worked away together. The car was bought for me when I was seventeen. It was the family car and it was a great thing that time to get a new car and I really appreciated it. It was the family car, the car to bring them to town or go to the doctor. It was also my car to go to the dance, which was important too. That was grand but he died suddenly when I was twenty. He got a massive heart attack in the bog and he never returned. That was a big blow to the whole place then. Mam was undecided what she'd do and I gave her the same promise that I gave Dad and she'll tell you to this day they were the happiest years of her life.

The place at home was a better farm than this one and it was easier to manage. I'm happy here but it took me a few years to settle down. My mother's partner left me this place. Hilly farming is harder. You are stuck in the rocks but still it's nice to be your own boss. I've a hundred and eight acres here. There were no fields when I came here that you could go into with a tractor and mower. It was very rough. We got a machine in and did a lot of reclaiming and took ditches away. Well it was only me here at the time but I had my nephew with me, a young fellow of seven or eight, picking stones. And I will say he was the best young fellow that ever stood on this land for working. I fell into a relationship with a partner down the road and we worked very happily together. I'd say he was a lot of the backbone to me doing work. He's the father of my second boy. My marriage did not work out. Ah sure, things happen. I have two lovely sons and I'm fierce proud of them. My elder boy is twenty-two and he is carpentering but he's going to Australia soon and I feel the place won't be right without him.

My second son is fourteen and going to town school and he's doing very well. He's an excellent student and he's gone to school eight or nine years without missing one day. If I was dead he wouldn't stay at home to bury me! I didn't like school and my eldest boy didn't either. It depends a lot on the teachers that's going today. He's fierce bright. It would be a shame if he doesn't go to college. Well, I think there's a great chance for him if he'd continue. He's not fond of it but he just does it and he's like the clock ticking, he's so organised. The two young fellows are like chalk and cheese. My eldest lad was on his own for so long he looked up to my nephews. He was kind of a man before his time and the same thing is happening now with the younger lad. He's looking up at being a man before his time because he's stuck in the shearing and he enjoys it as well. He has got two trophies for under-twenty-one shearing. It was a great satisfaction that they were that involved in it growing up. They weren't hanging round corners like town children. They can get up on the tractor and drive the jeep around the place. They have a fierce advantage over town children and they don't realise it or appreciate it.

One big change in farming is that you are not allowed to kill your own animals or fowl. There are all kinds of restrictions and red tape. If you were to kill your own animals now you'd have to send them to the slaughterhouse. Sure you're not even allowed to kill your own turkey or the auld goose. I don't know what the world is coming to. If a cow dies on your holding you'll have to get on to the Department and you'll pay €40 or €45 to take that animal off your land even though you are already at the loss of that dead animal. And you'll have to make sure that the paperwork is done right for accountability and traceability. The same thing for sheep – they're tagged and if one of them dies you'll have to pay to have them removed as well. I never have that opportunity because the foxes have them claimed before we'd get them dead. All you'd find is a fist of bones and you might be lucky to get the ear tag. The foxes do us a favour! That's the one good thing they do. At least we have our own produce. We know what we're eating. We have our deep freeze and it's great. You have fresh meat the day you want it.

Deer are getting popular here now. There are no boundaries really so they spread out and you have a lot of interbreeding. You have the red deer in the National Park in Killarney but you've sika as well and I'd say they're cross-bred enough. They're moving out all the time. At night now you'd hear them whistling. You can get a special licence to shoot the deer. You'd have to shoot them. They'd be knocking fences and eating grass. They'd eat as much as a cow.

The drink-driving laws now have changed rural Ireland and they are making people more isolated. You can't drive home. You've no choice now if you want to go out for a night. You have to hire a taxi to go out and get a taxi again to come home. If you're going to a wedding you drive over to Killarney and you stay in the hotel for the night but sure when you get up after a few drinks the following day wouldn't you love another drink but now you can't have that either because you need to drive home. And you can't drive home until evening. That's two days the wedding is going to take and the chances are you'll be caught coming home. So that's a dear wedding. The only time we go out now is for a bite to eat. We'd go out once in the blue moon. We'd go to Glengarriff to a restaurant and we might have one drink while we're waiting for the meal to be served us. I like the bit of music and dancing but sure you can't go in drinking minerals. I learned step-dancing when I was going to school long ago. You'd be able to do any dance after learning step dancing. I suppose it's three or four years ago since I actually danced a half-set or a polka. I wouldn't have the wind for it now or the fitness. I'm out of step. I'd still love to do it but sure we don't have that chance.

'I'd say I'm a dying tradition. Looking around me there isn't another woman doing what I'm doing in the locality.'

I have a nice modern kitchen here now but when I first took over this house there was nothing left in it only the four stone walls and half the roof – no running water, no electricity, nothing. It was unoccupied for four or five years. I lived here for about two years before I did anything. I couldn't afford to do anything. The biggest fear I had was that the rats would attack the young fellow in the cot. I got rid of the vermin with poison. We had to plaster the walls and put in new windows and doors. It was all one room so we started dividing it up. We had to dig our own well and the water in the taps now comes from our own well. We don't have any town supply. I'm two miles up from the main road. Our water is good and it makes a grand cup of tea. We got this tested and it's clear and beautiful. Well, the spring water is nicer.

'It is unreal to go out there in the night. You'd hear the fox barking and the deer whistling.'

I'd spend my life farming if I got my choice over again. There is no young one farming any more but it's a lovely life if you are cut out for it. I had a happy-go-lucky life in one sense but I think it was a mistake I didn't travel. I'm forty-seven now and I'm too old. My piece is over and done with. I have work to do. Once you have a child your life is cut and dried. I was in London once for a holiday and I didn't enjoy it at all. I'd hate to be inside in a town or a city. I'd sooner to be out. I don't know how the women today do it. I wouldn't give a child to anyone to babysit, not for long-term anyway. I might give it to someone for a couple of hours to mind it while I'm going somewhere. My mother gave me a great hand in rearing my child. I was backed a hundred per cent. A lot of people with mortgages in town haven't a choice. The only way they can have a roof over their heads is to have both of them working. I think it's wronging the children today that they don't know who the babysitter is who's minding them. I think it's very hard on the young children. They're growing up wild.

'There's way more work in sheep with dipping, dosing, shearing, marking and checking. They're a full time job. There isn't that much money out of them. And yet we pay such a high price for our lamb.'

Marie
McEnery

Marie McEnery (60) farms a large Friesian herd in Ballybunion with her husband and son. She worked for some years as a nurse in both England and Ireland before marrying Denis and settling in to fulltime farming. She comes from a farming background and milked by hand as a child. Now she is an expert with machines and all the technical aspects of modern farming.

I came from a farming background. When I was young we milked cows by hand because there were no machines at that time. My mother was not so hard on us but before we'd go to school in the morning she might ask us to milk a couple of cows. We learned to milk a cow with two of us sitting on a stool with the one bucket and we'd have two teats each. In years gone by our parents had to work very hard by comparison with nowadays. I mean open fires, having to light a fire in the morning and boil the kettle. I remember one time Yanks came to our house at home and I suppose my mother hadn't much in the house so she sent them away for a drive and told them to come back for their dinner. She went out in the yard, caught a chicken, plucked it and cleaned it and cooked it. We had new potatoes and cabbage and turnip out of the farm and she laid them up on the table in the parlour. When the Yanks came back she had a lovely dinner ready for them.

I left home when I was eighteen and it was after that they got a milking machine over at home. I met my husband Denis at a dance in Listowel when I was in Leaving Cert. I went off to England and did my nursing training. I was there for five and a half years and then I came back home and nursed in a nursing home in Listowel for a while. So we got married then.

I didn't do nursing after I married. I hadn't time, too busy with the farming. This was Denis's family farm here. His father and mother bought this place eighty odd years ago. Denis's father died when he was very young. He was only nine or ten. They never really knew what happened. His mother then had to rear them on her own and she worked as well milking cows. She died in 1954.

This was the old farmhouse when I first came to Dromin and the new house was built later. Denis's uncle was with us for a while. He had been a priest in America and he was with us for a few years before he died. No one lives in the old house now except for short terms. When relations or friends come they stay here. We have three children. Well Thomas didn't arrive for five years. I would take time out just to push him up town in the pram and show him off. Miriam arrived three years later and then we had Anne Maria five years later. I'd get them up in the morning, feed them and change them. I'd put them back again into their cot until I came back from the cows. Then I'd have to look after them again. Well I think that if you do nursing training you can face anything. There's no trouble giving them injections or anything. I'd give the cattle injections and look at the medicines more intently. I'd make sure the withdrawal period would be right. The men would too. We'd only ask the vet what would be recommended if they had pneumonia or something like that. We inject and give it ourselves because calling out the vet is expensive but one would buy the medicine from them.

My son Thomas is twenty-nine and single and he is running the farm now but he doesn't milk. He would in an emergency but that's all. He does all the other work now. He'll spread slurry and put out the fertiliser and help in the caravan park as well. Well he has the Green Cert now and that means that when we are signing over the farm to him he won't have to pay stamp duty. He went to Pallaskenry and then he went to college in England for a year. He does the farm accounts now. My daughter is actually doing the Green Cert course through Teagasc-on-line in Clonakilty. She goes to Clonakilty for a day with the group every few months. This course will be necessary if she gets the farm in Dun Ferris which has sixty acres. We have 196 acres but it is not all together.

We don't do any winter milk. We start drying the cows off around this time of the year now, September-October. They wouldn't have as much milk this time of the year except the few late calvers. We give them dairy nuts all the year round during their milking time. When they're dried off they just get silage. It's all Friesians we have here. We usually get up around seven in the morning, have a cup of tea and up to the yard. We have a very good workman. He's usually there early as well. He'd bring the cows from the fields and he'd change the fence. I usually start washing up the milking parlour from the night before, letting out the detergent because we leave it in all night to sterilise the equipment. I get all the equipment ready and we drive the cows in and out then. Tom and myself usually milk and two is enough in a milking parlour. We have twelve units so we can milk twelve cows each side. We milk about 120 or 130 cows. We scrub the passages and hose out the parlour and get it ready again for the evening. We come in then and clean ourselves up and have our big breakfast. We have porridge and then bread and an egg maybe. I bake my own bread. We start again around five o'clock in the evening.

It takes about an hour-and-a-half in the heavy times and about an hour when the cows are slackening.

If one sees anything wrong with the milk one does not put it into the tank. That has to be kept for the calves. If a cow has antibiotics we always have a mark on that cow so that any inhibitors won't be let into the tank. It has to be kept out for seventy hours. Then I write it into the herd register when we come in. In the herd register we also have to put in every new calf that's born, the date they're born and their breed, and the mother's number. They can come at any time and check your register. It applies to every animal. All cattle now have to be traced. All calves have to be tagged within about twenty days of being calved. Anything that's born on the farm or sold off the farm is registered and if we buy a cow that has to go into the register. I do the records and there is a good bit of bookwork.

'We learned to milk with two (?) us siting on a stool with one bucket and we'd have two teats each. In years gone by our parents had to work very hard by comparison with nowadays. I mean open fires, having to light a fire in the morning and boil the kettle.'

I kept hens but then the men couldn't have enough houses for cattle or calves! One day I had turkeys ready for Christmas and they wanted the house. Nothing would do them. They just wanted the house. So off I had to go and kill all the turkeys and pluck them and clean them and take them all off to Ballyroe Hotel in Tralee. I suppose there were twenty in it at that time and that was the end of poultry for me. I would love to have my own fowl again. I'd get day-olds then and rear them. People from the town would come here for the free-range eggs when I had them. If I'm in the shop I'll always buy free-range eggs.

I think it is a very satisfying life but you're tied seven days a week. If one goes anywhere one has to be back for the cows. There is the Farm Relief Scheme but we have never availed of it because we always have Tom who works with us. Our daughter married recently. We had the cows milked in the morning and that evening Tom milked them on his own. Farming has cleaned up a lot. It's much more hygienic now than it was. Modern regulations are not a bad thing. You know in years gone by milk was just put straight into a tank without being cooled and they'd throw buckets of water over the tank to cool it. I'm sure milk wasn't that fresh going to the creamery then because it was out in the heat. I remember buying butter at the creamery and my mother often had to send it back because it wouldn't be good. There would be a bad taste on the butter. So there's a lot to be said for today's hygienic requirements. The slurry and spreading regulations aren't too bad. It's an advantage for people with a smaller holding to be in REPS because you get a grant but you have to have a very tidy set-up. You have to have all the hedges cut. The roadways must be okay. There must be no rubbish around. I'd say the smaller holdings would be in it but the bigger holdings wouldn't. We're not in the scheme because we wouldn't get that much money. It's so much for the first twenty acres and so much then for the next twenty acres so that it would be decreasing all the time.

There is an inspection of the milking parlour from time to time to see that everything is OK. Somebody from the co-op comes out to see that everything is clean. We get the milking parlour serviced every year by Dairymaster. They go through the whole thing to see if everything is working and if rubbers need to be replaced. We have to replace the liners ourselves every year. It is better for the cows and it prevents mastitis. Denis reads the *Farmer's Journal* every week so he gets all the advice in that. We'd have somebody out now to test the milk and take a sample of milk maybe to see if the cattle are low in selenium, cobalt, or iodine and then they will advise us as to which boluses to use. If the year is bad they might be low in some things. We had our test done this year and they were a bit low on selenium so we're going to give the boluses now before they calve. If a cow is low on those things they can abort the calf or it can be weak after birth. Or they could retain the afterbirth and that would slow them down for going in calf the following year.

Our milk is collected every three days and tested for mastitis every time it is collected. The cell count has to be under 400 and it is tested for quality twice a month. We go through the cows and do our own testing. We have a kit called CMT and we can buy that at the co-op. We find this very good because our cell count is always under 400 and that is the

ideal. If a cow is high in cell count we don't let that cow's milk into the tank. We have recording jars and can see the milk before it is released into the tank. We keep it for the calves. You have to be wary because it could go up high unknown to you.

The hardest time is when the cows are calving. We have a monitor in the bedroom and we have a camera in the calving house and we can see the cow calving from the bedroom. Denis looks after the calving but if there is a problem all of us will go. We have a calving jack now. You put it on the cow and you lever the calf out if it's a difficult one but in years gone by when there was no calving jack people had to get a few neighbours and put a rope round the calf's front legs and pull it. It was very strenuous. That is the toughest time really. It is fine if they calf during the day but then at night you could have two or three cows calving. We bucket-feed everything. It is very time-consuming but you know what every calf is getting. We put them feeding on troughs when they get a bit bigger.

'I would love to have my own fowl again. I'd get day-olds then and rear them. People from the town would come here for the free-range eggs when I had them. If I'm in a shop I'll always buy free-range eggs.'

We have our own bulls because if we used the AI we would have to be watching the cows all the time and tail-painting them. We would have a variety of bulls. We could have a Friesian bull or a Simmental or a Charolais. We would have beef bulls and we keep the Friesian calves for replacements. We would sell off the beef calves. You wouldn't get that much for Friesian bulls. Charolais bulls go well with Friesian cows so there is a good bit of money to be made out of those calves.

Major decisions on the farm would be joint decisions. Well, the men do their own thing, looking after machinery and things like that. We have a joint account. If we get paid for the mart or anything like that I just lodge the money. When there's money needed for the running of the house I usually take it out. Thomas usually comes if he wants to buy machinery or buy cattle and I sign the cheque for him.

Looking back on it the farm was a great environment for bringing up children. I think country life was great for them. They did their own little jobs. As soon as they were able to they would hold a bucket and feed a calf. You knew they were not bored because they were involved with animals. Miriam and Anne Maria drove the tractor and the digger. They loaded cattle and brought them home and they took them from one farm to the other. As for the farm being continued into the next generation, it's getting less and less likely really. Even the farmers' daughters aren't inclined to stay at home farming now because they would be tied to it for seven days a week. They are not as interested. A lot of young farmers' sons sold their cows and went away and got jobs. While the building boom was there, there was good money in it. Some just have dry cattle now and are part-time farmers. For years there wasn't that much money in dairying but now things are turning around. I would like to see the farm continued. I love the farming. I think it is a great life and a nice healthy life too.

Outside of farming I have been involved in the ICA in Ballybunion for thirty-four years. We go to federation meetings. I'm on the committee in our locality and I've been treasurer and PRO. I'd be putting the notes into the paper letting people know what courses are going on in An Grianán. It's a great way to meet people. The ICA people are always a very friendly crowd and we are very close. We've had ICA outings to various parts of the country. We've had a few craft classes and we did Carrickmacross lace, ruck cushions, leather and sheepskin gloves. Some of our members have gone to An Grianán in County Louth, where they have done different courses there like cookery and embroidery.

'If a cow is low on those things they can abort the calf or it can be weak after birth. Or they could retain the afterbirth and that would slow them down for going in calf the following year.'

The younger women are joining other women's groups now and they have no voice. The next parish is Asdee. They have a women's group there. They just get together, organise outings and things like that but they have no voice in the government, whereas the ICA has. If you want to talk about drugs and different things like that you can have little discussions and the president can take it to the government. I think the younger women think that the ICA is just for sewing and crafts and things like that. For them there's no such thing as darning or sewing any more. The ICA has changed but the younger people don't know that. I mean the ICA is more involved in other things now.

'The ICA people are always a very friendly crowd and we are very close. We've had ICA outings to various parts of the country. We've had a few craft classes and we did Carrickmacross lace, ruck cushions, leather and sheepskin gloves.'

Apart from the ICA I go set dancing. During the winter we have set-dancing classes every week. It is very sociable. This year I started in Asdee. My husband doesn't dance but if you go to céilís you don't ever have to have a partner because you get plenty to dance with. It is not like ballroom dancing where you need a partner. The north Kerry set is the one we do. We learn a few new sets every year. There are well over a hundred set dances and I'd have a good idea of at least thirty. I wear black laced leather shoes for the set dancing. You get them in the Dance Shop in Cruise's Street in Limerick. They have all the dancing stuff there. The men have black shoes, usually leather shoes with real leather soles. For dancing shoes you have to have light leather soles to get around the floor. I have the laced-up ones like Granny used to wear and I have the ones with the little strap across and they have lovely soft leather. I just got the fancy ones for the World Fleadh in Ballybunion. We went set dancing every night during that week. I would also go to the All-Ireland Fleadh in Listowel and other parts of the country like Clonmel and Wexford.

When we are not so busy on the farm I love to go on holidays and travel with a group or with friends. We have been to the European Parliament and I went on Chriss Nolan's trip to Scotland twice on the Maurice Walsh Trail. We went to Cape Town in South Africa and I've been to the Holy Land with a group from Moyvane. I am very interested in country-and-western music so I went to Nashville last year to the Country Music Festival. The country music in Nashville is getting more modern, more like pop I suppose, but I preferred the bars where the older singers performed. We went to Memphis where Elvis Presley lived and to Loretta Lynn's place and Dolly Parton's. We went to Canada and New England another year and to Eastern Europe last year, which was interesting because we visited the concentration camps. Betty Hartnett and I go off by ourselves abroad and we usually join the group in that country. The next big trip is to Australia for three weeks and then on to New Zealand for two weeks. I love travelling and seeing new places at the quieter time of the year when farming is not so hectic.

'there are well over a hundread set dances and I'd have a good idea of at least thirty. I wear black laced leather shoes for the set dancing.'

Maria O'Connor

Maria O'Connor (63) is a sheep farmer in Kilmalkedar, Ballydavid, in the Dingle peninsula. Maria went from being an Eastender town girl in London to dairy farmer with her husband in his home place in the heart of the Kerry Gaeltacht where they reared their five daughters. With changing times she has seen the demise of dairy farming west of Dingle where most are now in part-time farming, raising sheep or dry cattle.

I was born in Tralee so I am a Kerrywoman and not a blow-in. People always thought I was a blow-in. Both my parents were Irish but my father had to go to England when I was quite young. My father worked in England most of his life and only ever came back once. He was from Muiríoch in the Dingle peninsula, so you could say I've come back. My mother was from Blennerville, Tralee. I grew up in the East End of London. I didn't ever think I'd be back in Ireland, even though as a child we came on holidays. I always liked Ireland. I left school very young, at fourteen. I wanted to be a nurse and Mum said to me, 'It's much too hard for you really.' I went into a factory where they used to make wedding dresses and I trained to be a flat machinist which was another name for a dressmaker. I did it for years and I really didn't like it but in those days you did it. It was a job. I was trained and earning good money. I always loved clothes and the fashion side of it and we could buy our dresses in there. After a while I left and got another job at Schubert's, a Jewish firm that made fantastic dresses and we could buy at wholesale. I met a lot of friends there and had great times working from age sixteen to twenty-one. It was a wonderful time. We would drink around the East End at The Blind Beggar, associated more often now with the infamous

Kray Twins. The 1960s were great. I saw the Beatles live in concert.

Mum and Dad were very good Catholics and always went to Mass on a Sunday. My aunt was a Bon Secours nun and she was in London. I went to Catholic dances, the church hall, but I was an East Ender really. I was maybe more English when I was in England and whenever I'd come back to Ireland I was only on holiday. It was a huge adjustment to come here to Ireland and get involved in farming but I was still quite young. I was thirty-two when I came back. Maybe I had a grá for the fields and the sea. I loved the area but the work I wasn't used to at all. It was a shock really.

I met my husband Tom going to Mass with my father in London. Tom was with a cousin of mine who had come over from Ireland. At Christmastime when the Irish fellows were over my mother would invite everyone to dinner. That's how I got to know Tom. We knew each other from when I was fifteen and I was married at twenty-one, in 1966. Tom's father died and he inherited the farm from his father so we decided to come back here. That was in 1978. We had three children at the time, aged seven, nine and eleven. Tom had been in construction work and had done quite well. He went into the haulage business and had a few trucks on the road and we had a little bit of money set aside. We sold our house in Illford in Essex and decided to come back and go into dairy farming. We had only the grass of eight cows and I remember his uncle said at the time, 'I don't know Tom. Maybe you should go into your trucks.' At the time he had brought back a machine and Tom said, 'No, I'm going to build a milking parlour. This is what I really want to do.' The land was very stony and boggy and he reclaimed a lot of it and worked very hard. We have roughly 120 acres of land, mostly mountain. We have sheep on the mountain and we had cows when we came back from England.

Well, all our money went into it. We built a milking parlour, went really modern, putting up the sheds outside for silage and a lean-to. We borrowed £10,000 from the bank and it took us such a long time to pay that back. That was in 1979. Interest rates went up so a lot of people who borrowed lost their farms. We were lucky. That was the only money we ever borrowed.

We did all the milking by machine. The regulations in those days were tough enough. We had to get hot water and things went sky-high and there wasn't anybody coming in to train us either. It was all strange to us but we had the three children. We were very close and worked hard together from seven in the morning until eight at night. The girls were great. We trained Helena and if we wanted to go to a wedding or somewhere else they could milk. We'd come back that night. Very seldom we'd stay away. I had all girls and they were very good and they loved animals. It was all strange to them. We never encouraged them to go into farming because the work was too hard and we wanted them to have an education. There was only a living for one family. Financially it wasn't the way to go. It was too small. We only barely survived.

We started with fifteen cows and then went up to twenty. Tom kept reclaiming the land and working very hard. We'd employ somebody sometimes and we set our own potatoes. We had our own lamb. Really it was just go, go, go. We finally came up to thirty-two cows. We leased the milk quota and we

were paying that back to Kerry Co-Op, which was expensive. By the time our cheque would come in it would barely keep us for the month because I had no other job. It needed the two to work together. I always stayed at home with the kids even when I was in London.

We were in dairying right up until 2002, over twenty-five years side by side working together until we finally got out of it. It really wasn't viable. We should have got out a lot sooner. We sold two sites to keep our three girls in college. They got the small Gaeltacht grant and it didn't pay a lot. They all did quite well really. I had my other baby, Angela, after eleven years, and then I had Eilís after that. I kept trying for this boy but he did not come. The girls had a lot of farming experience. Each one of them could milk cows and help on the farm. It's a wonderful life really. They all say it was wonderful because they worked and picked stones. When Dad was reclaiming land he'd say, 'We'll pick stones for two hours and then you can go to the beach.' I always took them to the beach in summertime when they had finished work. Everyone would pull their weight and make the sandwiches and we'd be back at half past five to milk the cows again. They'd go for the cows. It was just a whole family business.

When we were in London I would always bring them home to Ireland. Helena, the eldest, always loved coming on holidays. I'd drive across on the ferry and bring them home so they kind of had got used to it and they would hate going back to London. I had no proper education myself and I really wanted them to do better than I did. It was me that was pushing all the time. Tom was different. He wouldn't care what they'd be. 'Let them do what they want to do,' he'd just

say, but I bought books and books, and we'd go to the library. And they read every Enid Blyton book and every book that was going. In Ballydavid we had no television. They were working outside and they were playing basketball, football and swimming. I had to drive them to activities all the time. We had brought home an old jeep. The kids were dressed like city slickers and when we went to Mass the first time somebody said, 'Are they the Royal Family'? It was a change for them as well. They were eleven, ten and seven but they adjusted very easily even to the Irish language. There was no problem. They went to Clochar na Toirbhirte (Presentation convent) in Dingle town and Sister Mary was wonderful. I was worried about the Irish but she said to me, 'We have a teacher here and she'll take the children out.' They had an extra hour for Irish every day. People came into the house here and Tom always spoke Irish and they picked it up pretty fast. Tom is a fluent Irish speaker. I have the cúpla focal. They'd laugh at me when I'd speak it. Three of them have degrees. Angela teaches in a Gaelscoil. Eilís has Irish but she's doing public relations. She's the baby. Siobhán did marketing and Bernie did travel and tourism. I always wanted them all to have that bit of paper – that was my dream.

I have no regrets about bringing them back to Ireland. They say themselves that they had everything in their childhood and upbringing and following the animals. They had everything without television. I think contact with nature is a great way to bring children up. They see so much. They see cows having calves. It's a whole sex education really on the farm. It was great. They lived with death as well, seeing animals dying, the cycle of life. We had two or three dogs.

Helena had a pet rabbit as well. She was really the one for the animals. The rabbit got out of the cage one day and we had greyhounds at this stage and that was it, end of rabbit. Thomas had the greyhounds. We had a couple of winners but there was no money in it and it was time-consuming to go all the way into Tralee with the two greyhounds. That was another funny story. We got a guy down here to train them. He had the greyhound for about a week and he said, 'I'm sure there's something wrong with the greyhound. I was watching him the other day doing his business and this thing came out from inside and I don't know what it was'. He put it in the bag and brought it up to Tom. This was a local farmer. He probably had never seen corn on the cob before. It was his first time to see corn on the cob west of Dingle.

'I had all girls ... We never encouraged them to go into farming because the work was too hard and we wanted them to have an education.'

When we got out of dairy farming it was because of the hardship and Tom was getting that little bit older. We were working for nothing so we decided we'd tone down a little bit. The girls had gone off doing their own thing and we went into sheep. Well we had always maybe forty or fifty sheep on the mountain. We are full-time sheep farmers now and it is hard work again. You have to check them. We have a couple of hundred sheep on the mountain and on the lowland then as well. It just keeps us ticking over with all the girls gone. We have Suffolk and Scotch mostly.

We are very busy in the lambing season from St Patrick's Day up to about the end of May. I've always gone to the mart but I'd let Tom do the selling. I wouldn't do it. I suppose I'm old fashioned maybe – a kid from the city. When you're involved in the farm it's hard going. Women see themselves as having to do the house and the farm. Farm men tend to do the farmwork. Tom is wonderful but he's better working outside and he works very hard. He would do the housework if I go to London. Again he always had the girls so he had a lot of women around.

I suppose we always worked together. We always had the joint cheque book. There was no question of money. When we were dairy farming I was very lucky that my mother was in London and she was very good to me. She would go out and buy stuff. She was a giver. At Christmas time she'd send parcels of clothes so I was one of the lucky ones. At Easter and Christmas she'd send sterling. She used to feel sorry for me. At the beginning she said, 'What are you going back there for? It's crazy.' She hated it although she was brought up on a small farm. In later years when the city changed and as she got older I think she thought I made a good choice. As for my father I'd say he was devastated. He only came over once to visit here. Well, he liked Tom but he just thought it wasn't the place for his daughter. He remembered when he was a boy in Muiríoch and he had to leave for work. Before he went to London he worked for big farmers in Tralee and he always looked at the poverty west of Dingle. It wasn't a place where you could make a living. I think when he came back and saw the milking parlour and what we had achieved he was surprised. He was proud and I was glad because two years later he died. Emigration then was either to America or England. I did the reverse. All his brothers and sisters went to America. He was the one who went to England and very few came back. They didn't want to come back. You were coming back to poverty and you wanted to forget.

What we had in London was a council flat and my father thought it wonderful for an Irishman to have a council flat in the East End. That was big. He worked in construction for McAlpine all his life. He thought Tom was crazy for coming back to the farm. Tom had a lot of friends in construction and some had got very rich and we left and came back here and they would visit us. They would say, 'What are you doing here?' And we'd say, 'We're here for the quality of life and the children as well.' When I look back at some of my friends in London I think mine had a better childhood, more quality of life and better education as well. I've no regrets. It was wonderful. I'd say I was never materialistic so that was a bonus. My kitchen is the same as it was thirty years ago. I always liked old-fashioned stuff. I would go round to second-hand shops and pick up chairs and pots and things. I was really into old things. Management of money was one thing we never argued over because we didn't have a lot. We had thrown everything into the farm.

I did the accounts. Tom would just let me do it. He'd get the meal and stuff and I'd be balancing the books. I was good at managing really. Tom would do the farm register for the sheep. Tom used to shear but he wouldn't now. His back isn't great. We get someone to shear and that doesn't pay any more because the price of wool wouldn't even cover the cost of shearing. That's gone. I'd say only for the subsidies and the area aid there isn't any money or a future in sheep farming. What you get for a lamb and then go in and see the price of a lamb – definitely not. The middleman gets that money. You would have no living around here in sheep anyhow, only for the subsidies and the area aid and REPS as well.

'I'd say only for the subsidies and the area aid there isn't any money or a future in sheep farming. What you get for a lamb and then go in and see the price of a lamb - definitely not. The middleman gets that money.'

We're kind of thinking about going organic. We take ours to the mart and we sell them there. You'd have to be organic to sell to a butcher but there's a little bit more money in it. I mean Tom is sixty-five and I'm sixty-three coming up. There are a couple of more years in us and we love doing it. If it would pay at all we'd like to keep doing it. We have five daughters and they all love the land but what do you do when you have five daughters? Are you going to give it to one? They all have their own lives. Tom wants to give them all sites so they all have a site here. Helena is building at the moment. The way life is going this farm could be paying for our nursing home. I don't think I'd have my daughter taking care of me. We took care of my mother and I think it was hard work. I wouldn't want my girls to do it. I think I'd put myself up somewhere.

It was a great life. I enjoyed it. I enjoyed farming. I really did. I'm still enjoying it without the money. I like outdoor life. I like being able to walk out the fields with animals. I think you have to like animals. There are very few young women in it and if so they are working full-time at another job. I can't see it going back to how it was.

Because our farms are west of Dingle it will always be part-time farming. It will never be like it was with the whole family, husband and wife working the farm. For dairy farming you need a lot of land. Ours is too boggy. Mostly it wouldn't be great. You'd get big farms the other side of Dingle. Here in Baile na nGall it would be more sheep farming or dry cattle. When we were dairy farming there were a hundred dairy farmers going to Ballyferriter. Every year the numbers were going down and there isn't a dairy farmer in Muiríoch or Ballydavid now. I think there's one in Feothanach. There are very few in Ballyferriter. I'd say in a five-mile radius there's only one and they'd have about thirty or forty cows. They'd be just lucky. So many farmers here have sold sites for houses and we did also – otherwise we wouldn't have survived. We'll survive now because we've reared our children.

Well we're kind of lucky here. We have a lot of archaeological sites on our land. St Brendan's church is on our land. It's a ruin now. A couple of years ago St Brendan's graveyard was getting full and the county council came to Tom and said they wanted a new graveyard and asked if he'd sell a piece of land to them. He did and after a while Kerry County Council agreed on a small amount of money. I was delighted that he sold it because I said it will be a great privilege for us to be buried on our own land. There have been six or eight of the O'Connors on this farm. Tom can go back about seven generations. My own people on my parents' side are buried in St Brendan's. My father was brought back from England. They'd be in the old graveyard. The new graveyard has a lovely sea aspect. It's a nice idea to be buried on your own land. Well it's Kerry County Council's land but it was originally ours.

When the kids were young the social life here was much better. You'd have a mart social maybe once a year. That was the meeting place. You got dressed up and had dinner and dancing. A lot of big stores and the GAA would have them as well. There were lots of benefit dances. If somebody died or there was a tragedy people would have dances and gather money. People still hadn't television and we were here for nearly ten years without it. We had a lovely social life for the first fifteen years when we came back from London. There was a lot going on. I would go to the creamery and I'd leave Tom at home. We had a little bulk tank on to the back of the car. That was great but that vanished then after about ten years and they put in the big cooler and the bigger tank so you didn't have to go to the creamery any more.

I'd say social contact is waning in the community and in farming generally. People don't talk about farming any more. There are fewer farmers. In our village now there are three sheep farmers but they're getting older. Their children are part-time farmers. It wouldn't be the focus any more, not here anyway. They have other jobs. The whole fabric of rural Ireland with the farm at the centre has changed. We're here

thirty years and it has changed so much. Oh my God, sad changes, but there are more houses, which is nice for young people. They don't have to emigrate any more. There are a lot of holiday homes. Many people want to live in the Dingle peninsula and a lot of people from the cities bought sites from the farmers. It was much nicer when everyone was farming I think because there weren't as many houses.

Mary Quilter

Mary Quilter (90) lives in Scartaglen with her daughter and son-in-law. She has seen many changes in farming over the years, from hand-milking with the bucket and three-legged stool to the modern era of the milking machine. Mary has been widowed for many years and lives a very active life today, getting up early for daily Mass, socialising and doing her exercises with Active Retirement and playing cards at night. She is a great believer in fitness for mind and body.

I wasn't always in farming. Before I married, my father and mother had a shop about half a mile away from where I'm now at this present moment. My mother was a midwife. I didn't move very far then. I loved school. We went through the fields barefoot and we made our own path with the passing of time. In those days, clothes such as home-knit jumpers, cardigans and socks would have been passed on from the older children to the younger ones. I had farming experience before I got married because we had a few cows at home, just a few. I was involved in looking after them and I milked by hand at home as a child.

I met my husband Batty Quilter in the shop. He was a customer in the shop. I chose him myself! We married in 1939 and I went into this farm. We were very happy, which was a very important thing. Sure he spoilt me. He wouldn't allow me do too much. I got no spoiling at home but I did then when I married. He had a two-storey house and there were always two candles lighting in it. Times were hard but we were happy. I retired only a few years ago so I had a very long farming career. I live here now in this bungalow with my daughter and her husband. The farmhouse where I lived my married life is up the road there. My daughter held on to it for years and now her daughter and her husband have taken over. My granddaughter is now doing dairying full-time and she has four kids. It keeps her going.

I have seen many changes in my time but the biggest one was the milking machine. Before that I, like so many more at that time, had to milk cows by hand and that was a skill in itself. We took no notice of it because everybody else was doing the same. You'd have a bucket and you sat on a three-corner stool with a lantern to aid vision early in the morning or in the dark winter evenings. The hands had to move in a certain way and you had to be careful in case the cow would kick. Hand-milking was a very laborious task. There was a lot to be done. My husband would get on to his knees in the morning and say his prayers before he'd go out milking. The cows would have to be driven in to the cowhouse and tied up. We had two men working and they would milk too. We'd have ten to twelve cows morning and evening. After the milking we'd put the milk into the churns. You had to wash the churns by hand and scald them with boiling water to keep them clean. That was hard work but we loved it.

Most farmers had to get up at five in the morning to start the milking to get to the creamery on time. The day's work didn't finish until ten o'clock at night in the busy season and if there was a cow calving the farmer would have to rise during the night again. They would go to the creamery with the horse and cart and some had a pony and cart. Our workmen always did that. And they wouldn't go at all if they weren't the first at the creamery. They wanted to have a chat there with the neighbouring farmers. Meeting people at the creamery was a big social thing then. That's what they miss nowadays. They say farmers are very isolated and it's quite true.

Before the creamery started we made butter. You'd separate the milk and you'd have the cream then. You had a little machine for separating the milk from the cream. You made the butter in a churn and it was sold. You'd keep your own amount, about five pounds for the week. I was very good at it. The creamery came then and it was a great change and a relief. Before that you didn't go to the creamery with the milk. You'd be at the butter at home. When the creamery came you were selling the milk. We went to the creamery and we sold the milk there and got the creamery cheque. When we were doing the butter we'd get the messages right away in the shop where we'd sell it but it was different with the creamery cheque. That came once a month. You'd get your things on credit and pay for them later.

As well as looking after the cows I had to tend to turkeys, hens and pigs. The land was too dry for ducks. I raised all those fowl and fed them here myself. We kept some of the eggs for ourselves and we sold some as well. You'd only keep the hens for about two years and then you'd have the small ones, the chickens, coming on again. I didn't kill the old ones. At that time somebody would come and take them away. I don't know what he did with them but you'd be glad to get rid of them after rearing the chickens. If you didn't want the hens to hatch you'd put them under a pot to get the broodiness off them and you'd leave them there for a few days. You wouldn't feed the hen at all while she was under the pot and when she'd come out the broodiness would be gone and she'd start laying

away again.

We kept pigs as well and sold them. We'd have about three sows and they'd have banbhs a couple of times a year. I didn't ever stay up at night with them. That was always the men's job. We'd keep back a pig for ourselves and kill it at home. A neighbour would do the killing. He would go around to different places. That was his job. After the pig was killed you would salt it and put it into a tub. We'd keep the blood and we'd make puddings with it. I made puddings too. You would scrape the gut to make the puddings. Usually you'd take it to the river barefoot and give it a good wash and scrape it afterwards with a knife. You would know when it was ready when you could see clearly through it. If the gut became transparent it was ready for pouring the blood into it. It was in salt and water if it was done properly. It was an art in itself. At that time you divided the puddings and some of the pork steak with all the neighbours. How much they'd get depended on how many were in the house. If there were four or five you gave so many slices. At times you wouldn't have anything left for yourself but then you'd get it back when their turn would come around.

We planted potatoes as well, or spuds as we used to call them. I was good at cutting the sciolláns or seed potatoes. First you had to halve the potato and take a little piece off the edge of it. Sometimes you could have three out of a big potato. You'd have the eyes on the potatoes. Eight or nine or ten would grow from every seed potato then. Usually the eldest person in the house would do the cutting. They were probably the most experienced. That was interesting. When it came to setting the potatoes it was mostly the man's job. If the stalk was too high this meant that the potato was not properly set. I never did it anyway. The men would dig them and pit them. You'd have pits seven or eight feet long. You'd cover them with earth. There were usually rat-traps around them. We never had rats because we had the cats around. You'd need them. In the vegetable garden too we grew cabbage, onions and carrots and I enjoyed doing that.

'I was good at cutting the sciollāns or seed potatoes. First you had to halve the potato and take a little piece off the edge of it. Sometimes you could have three out of a big potato. You'd have the eyes on the potatoes.'

My husband did the ploughing himself with horses. We had four horses. Two horses would plough up to dinner hour and then the other two horses would be put in to give the first two a rest. There was no mention of the man. He had to keep going all day. All the pity was for the horses. The workmen never did the ploughing. There was a knack in setting the plough and they wouldn't have any experience of it. I don't know any workman who did it. There was a real art in ploughing with horses and keeping the plough straight. My husband prided in his ploughing anyway. Some people were not so good at it.

The men went to the bog cutting the turf but I never went.

They cut it by hand with a sleán. It was hard work. You'd want three for the cutting of the turf, one to cut it, one to throw it out and then another person to throw it further on. It had to be stooked and stacked after that when it was dry. The men did that all the time. We burned all our own turf and trees. There were no chainsaws there that time. You had to cut the wood with an axe. It was in later years that you had a chainsaw.

I loved the hay and my favourite job was raking it with the wheel rake and the horse. No matter how quick he'd go I was still quicker. That was a tricky enough job now. I'd be in a hurry out to be helping and I'd work away in the sun. I'd be on the rake before anybody, preparing it for the wynds. I never made the wynds. That was the men's job. When they'd make the wynds then they would twist the súgán. They had this gadget and they'd keep twisting the hay around it to make a long rope. They'd put it across the wynd and tie it down at the bottom and crosswise then. They had to put two súgáns on each wynd. There was an art in that too. There was an art in everything if you like. Then they would bring it home on a float. Some people called it the hay-car. You twisted it up on the float with a handle and brought it into the shed. And it was all hand work.

During my time on the farm we never had a tractor. My husband died suddenly but by then we had retired. I continued doing a lot of farming jobs. I stayed at it all the time. We had got the milking machine before he died. I was able to work the milking machine and I loved it. I'd be able to put on the clusters and milk the cows on my own if I had to. If the need arose that the men wouldn't be around or if they were gone to the bog or other things I could do it. I saw the whole transition from the hand-milking right into the milking machine. We had the bulk tank then. The milk wasn't collected at all. You had to bring your own bulk tank to the creamery. So you'd still meet up with the farming men. Later still the milk lorry would come to collect the milk. You'd miss it a lot now because the man collecting the milk would come in and sit down for half an hour and we'd hear all the news. He'd have tea when he'd come and tea when he'd go. There was plenty of time then. They have no time now. Nowadays the man collecting milk wouldn't be allowed in. He has to account for his time, which is a pity.

I knitted as well but only very little, just a bit to pass away the night. I would knit jumpers and socks. At that time it was all knitted socks. You would learn to turn the heel and close the toe. Wearing them on a farm, I think, was a pure waste of time. You had to darn them so much. They would wear very quickly, the wool sock anyway. They were comfortable with a strong shoe, that's the only thing. There was quite an art in darning too as well as knitting. We were taught that at school. They don't do any of that now. Any of us don't.

'I never made the wynds. That was the man's job. When they'd make the wynds then they would twist the súgán. They had this gadget and they'd keep twisting the hay around it to make a long rope. They'd put it across the wynd and tie it down at the bottom and crosswise then. They had to put two súgáns on each wynd. There was an art in that too.'

The day of the threshing was a big day for all the farmers. There would be about twelve people around, all of them neighbours. They'd all come together and we looked forward to it. It took two days usually but it could go on for about a week or more. Then it would be the neighbour's turn and it could be on for maybe a couple of weeks and they'd usually be a dance the night it ended. That was great fun. That was where the young women would meet their men. There was a watchful eye kept on them, too much sometimes. The local priests would keep a big eye on the young women at the dances in those days. They were strict, very strict and you know it would finish up at ten o'clock at night.

On the whole now I think religious devotion is coming back again. People are going here and there to shrines and prayer meetings. There are prayer meetings around here. In our parish church in Scartaglen there is a prayer meeting on the third Sunday of every month. It starts about a quarter to three and it's over at half-past five. The Rosary was very important in all houses one time. I hope it's being said all the time. It is a pity if it isn't. I'd be afraid to judge but it doesn't look like it is. Well, everyone has their own way of going to God.

I have a very active life now. I'm involved in Active Retirement. I go to Scartaglen in the morning around eleven and stay there until one. We have a lovely hall there now and we do all the exercises, arms up, heel, toes and all. It keeps me fit. It's a great help. The men don't go. It's on in Castleisland outside the town from two to half-past five. I go to that one as well. It's a pity they are both on the same day. I get a double dose of exercise in the one day. I'm not the eldest going there now. A lot of them are older and all are women.

I play cards every Monday night at Currans. I don't think I'd know the days of the week if I didn't go on a Monday night. I play whist. It's very good for the brain because you have to keep track of thirteen cards and the thirteen cards of your partner as well. That's twenty-six cards. But you'd always have some stake. Only a little bit of money changes hands but it's very good for the brain and it keeps me young at heart. I have been playing cards all my life. I played over at my own home. That would be the game called thirty-one. My father was an awful man for cards. It was handed down to me.

'I saw the whole transition from the hand-milking right into the milking machine. We had the bulb tank then. The milk wasn't collected at all. You had to bring your own bulk tank to the creamery.'

I get up every morning without fail at half-past eight. I have a shower, say a few prayers, have my breakfast, and then I go to eleven o'clock Mass in Castleisland six days a week.

My daughter and her husband take me to Mass. They go every morning as well. There would be a lot of people at that weekly morning Mass in Castleisland. So I have something to get up for every morning. I can read today without glasses and I don't wear any. I can do without them. I'm in great health thank God.

Pádraig O'Keeffe
Scartaglen Fiddler

Helen Ryan

Helen Ryan is in her mid-fifties and has a suckler herd at Direen, Mastergeehy, near Waterville. A mother of five, she came reluctantly to farming but discovered her hidden talents when she took over the family farmstead. She has travelled widely and lived in Canada before finding her niche in her home place in Direen where she lives with her husband Michael.

I had absolutely no interest in farming when I was growing up. When I was a child I suffered a lot from asthma so I tended to stay indoors and do the housework while my mother and sisters were out helping my father. I liked the radio and I could read whenever I got a chance. My father worked with the forestry so his farming tended to be from four o'clock in the afternoon onwards. When I left here I was about sixteen. This is my family home. I was born in the house across the road which is my father's house. I don't know how long my family has been farming here but I know they were here in 1825, according to *King's History of Kerry*. My mother was a local as well. When we came along there was no money really at the end of the 1950s. It was a dreadful time in Ireland and when the forestry started my father worked with them. So my mother ran the farm. At that time I think we had seven dairy cows. She was always involved out of doors and indoors. There were elderly people around as well. My grandfather and my granduncle lived here when I was young. We had a local school here at the time but that closed down eventually.

I went to the vocational school in Cahirciveen for two years and I left here because I got a kind of a scholarship, an apprenticeship basically from Gaeltarra Éireann as they were known at the time. They are now Údarás na Gaeltachta. I went off to west Galway for two years to school. We did typing, shorthand, arts and crafts, book-keeping and the usual academic subjects. I worked with Gaeltarra then for at least another two years. It was grand but the wages were very low. The first year after I finished school I worked in a knitwear factory in Tuar Mhic Éadaigh where the handknitters all over the Donegal and Mayo and Galway Gaeltachts sent their Aran sweaters. I worked in the quality control there for a year. An office job came up so then I went to Baile Bhúirne in the west Cork Gaeltacht where there was a textile factory opening at the time. That was in 1969 I think. I did book-keeping and office work generally for a year. Again the money was bad. We were getting something like ten guineas a week at the time and you had board and lodgings to pay out of that. I decided I would leave and I went to Dublin where I did office work in five or six different places. I met my husband-to-be in Dublin around 1972 and we went out together for two years. We decided after we got married that we were going to emigrate. He is from Dublin and was studying accountancy at the time. We got married in October 1974 and we headed off to Canada. He got a job as an internal auditor and I got a job with an insurance company in Vancouver for a while. We stayed for six months in Vancouver.

It rained for the whole summer of 1975 and the following winter we decided we would try the snow so we moved inland to Edmonton, Alberta. The snow was a novelty there for a while. We arrived in November and after Christmas I discovered I was pregnant. I got a job with the local government there, office work again. Ciara, our first child, was born in September 1976. The two years weren't quite up but we decided that we would come home. We were in a city-centre apartment where we weren't supposed to have kids anyway. Ciara was nine weeks old when we came back.

Kerry Group was setting up at the time. There was a lot of coverage in the press about them. Michael did an interview with them and got a job in the milk factory in Listowel. It produced milk, butter and cheese at the time. We bought a house in Tralee then and we stayed there for five years. Owen and Siobhán were born in Tralee. Orla was actually born in Tralee as well, then we moved back here. We decided we were going to move out of the town at that stage. I had done the birthday party thing a few times and I decided I could not stick this for the next ten or fifteen years. I'd go mad. I remember eleven girls rampaging through the house at Ciara's sixth birthday. My parents were living here at the time and they were getting old and they wanted out of the farming. My three sisters had all married at that stage and none of them was interested in farming and I wasn't particularly interested either. I think I felt somebody had to come back to look after the parents as they got older. We moved back here with four kids in June 1984. Initially I thought I would grow my own food and the kids would be better off with a bit of freedom in the country. The local school, Cillín Liath National School, is two miles down the road and it's a Gaeltacht school. Classes were small so I was happy enough about that.

Michael travelled quite a bit back and forth to America because Kerry Group was setting up operations over there. We decided to buy a second farm in the early 1990s. We built the slatted shed and we were expanding cow numbers. Roisín was born then in 1987. Michael has never really worked full-

time in farming. He is still in Kerry Group so he travels back and forth still. I did most of the farming with the help of casual labour when I could get it. It was difficult enough at the beginning coming back and getting people used to the idea of a woman farming. They reckoned: a few months of this will sort her out and she'll be off again. But I'm still here. I obviously knew more about farming than I realised. My husband, being a Dublin man, wouldn't have known anything, but that's not to say that he doesn't help on the farm. He has calved cows and he will do whatever has to be done. He is brilliant really because if I was out on the farm at weekends he would be in here and he would do the cooking.

At the beginning being a woman in a man's world was a bit traumatic. It is a male-oriented scenario. It was a world I didn't really enjoy being in but it was something I had to do so I went ahead and did it. It worked. I found most people extremely helpful. Well they would deal with you the same as a man after they figured out you weren't a total idiot and if they figured out that you knew what you were on about.

It was difficult to get back then because everyone was emigrating in the 1980s. It was beef production basically. Originally we went into sheep and we discovered very quickly there was no money in sheep so we gave that up. There is a lot of work in sheep especially lowland sheep and my son Eoin was helping out on the farm. I decided that he needed to go to college and get himself an education in case the farming thing wasn't his cup of tea. He went to Gorteen in Tipperary for his agricultural course. The devil himself can't shift him out of the place now and he's doing most of it. My mother died then in 1988 and my father was left on his own in the house across the road. He was in his eighties at that stage so we sort of managed this house and his house. We decided to build a slatted shed then. We went into the beef. We got Limousin cattle and it progressed from there. We bought the farm in Waterville and apart from the problems that go with fragmented farming it was grand. The quality of the land around here isn't great. We have about 300 acres now but it is mixed land. There's a lot of boggy marginal land in it. My son has reclaimed a lot of the last farm we bought and made a decent farm out of it.

'We are looking for a way to use up our marginal land so we are hoping to go into energy crops of some kind, and we would gladly produce something like Miscanthus grass. It is an energy source and it is supposed to grow well in boggy land so we are going to do a trial.'

When I came back here the cattle bred mostly were the traditional breeds and the Charolais. Everybody was on about the Charolais but the marketplace was demanding something different. We were producing Limousins and the calves or the sucklers tend to be that bit smaller when they're young.

People couldn't understand why we weren't doing Charolais but we used to sell the Limousins for more money at the time. If you bred good cattle people were prepared to pay the price. I always brought them to the mart and sold them for the best price available. I would leave my husband to do the negotiating if we needed loans in the bank or anything like that because being an accountant he would be better versed at dealing with that sort of thing. The bank account is in joint names so if I wanted money I never had any problem. In my mother's case now she always handled the finances in the house simply because my father never wanted to know about it really. My background was farming and men tended to fit the stereotypical role. They went out and did the work and my mother did whatever had to be done, whether it was caring for the elderly or cooking the dinner or feeding the cows. She would have turned her hand to any aspect of farming and the management or it. My father couldn't care less. He did a day's work and he'd come in and read his newspapers. I suppose that's where I got my reading thing from.

We brought up five children here on the farm and whatever was going on they mucked in. We bought two horses for them because they liked horse-riding but when they all left home they left me with the horses and cleaning out after them. I felt I had enough of that so we don't do horses any more. They have all got their degrees and I didn't press them academically. I have always had reservations about the points system, not the system itself but I don't think a kid should study to the exclusion of whatever else is going on around them. They need to be part of the world that they are growing up in.

At the minute now we have just been released from being closed down with TB. We were closed down all this summer. Eoin has about sixty-two cows and he is aiming to increase it. We run it as a partnership. He is out contracting because of the cash scenario basically. Anyone who knows anything about farming will know that there's little enough cash in it. Apart from doing the books I keep an eye on things while he's out. I like going out in the morning and walking around checking animals and he feeds them when they are in the shed. It's easier during the winter. There were times when it was quite difficult in the sense that I had to do the physical work like piking out silage out of bales in the shed but I don't do that any more. Eoin went to college and he did a degree in psychology. Well he came back and he just took up farming and he loves it. He didn't really want to go and practise at anything else. I think he's the sort who would only ever work for himself. He is happier working on his own.

'I don't see the logic in us producing food to very high standards when you can bring in food from Argentina or Brazil that we know hasn't been reared to the same high standard... Adaptability is the key if energy crops or something like that could come.'

We have suckler cows now. We are looking for a way of using up our marginal land so we are hoping to go into energy crops of some kind, and we would gladly produce something like miscanthus grass. It is an energy source and it is supposed to grow well in boggy land so we are going to do a trial. Eoin is going to put in an acre or two of it in the near future and see how it goes. We are getting advice from one of the energy companies. I got a lot of help from Teagasc too over the years. Generally speaking we would put sheep on marginal land around here but there is really no money in sheep. There is a lot of labour involved. If something else comes up we will probably try it. A lot of farmers are looking at alternative enterprises. I was hoping that the organic thing would take off because I think we will go back to producing on a small scale again on farms, maybe cheese or ducks or whatever people need. At the moment I keep a couple of hens and we do a garden for our own use too. To some extent we eat our own produce. In the early years I was so busy with kids and the main farm that I didn't get the chance to do much in the way of food but we always did a certain amount. I think I will put up a tunnel now and start again and produce more of my own food. We eat our own beef and the odd lamb. If you were to produce food here to bring to markets elsewhere distance is a problem. There is an hour of travelling to get out of the place and our road structure is not the greatest. The nearest organic market would be in Milltown and the nearest cattle marts are in Cahirciveen or Castleisland.

My son feels as I do really that you have to be adaptable. Farming as we know it is going to change. I don't know how much longer we'll be in beef if the CAP (Common Agricultural

Policy) or the world trade situation continues as it is because we're overwhelmed with EU rules. There is a lot of extra work. The paperwork is the biggest crib basically. Eoin has his records on the computer. I have my records in a book. In terms of registering animals it is not the most reliable way. We are smothered with rules. Meanwhile you have people bringing in beef from Brazil. I'm not terribly opposed to world trade or free trade because I realise everybody has to have their share of the cake but I don't see the logic in us producing food to very high standards when you can bring in food from Argentina or Brazil that we know hasn't been reared to the same high standard. If we felt it was we wouldn't crib really but traceability is a major problem. Adaptability is the key if energy crops or something like that could come. Otherwise the alternatives are artisan stuff, producing some aspect of food that people are prepared to buy.

We are forced to accept subsidies at the minute because there isn't a decent price for animals. That will be changed again and decreased probably and if the price of beef doesn't improve it's a sort of bleak outlook. Well I wouldn't say farming will be wiped out because there were terrible shenanigans in the dairy industry a few years ago. They thought they were being wiped out but now the thing has come full circle and they are talking about scarcities of milk so there is a possibility that some day down the road someone will appreciate good beef grown on grass again. So we are hoping that things will change.

I keep telling my son he's got to find himself a wife and let me get out of here and do something else with my life when I retire but he's not too enthusiastic. I wouldn't like to get out of it altogether but I'd absolutely love to go to Dublin now and again. I'd love to go to theatre or the city or even go shopping without stress. I go shopping to Tralee at the moment. What I miss are my closest friends that I've met over the years. I try to get away three or four times a year. I'm rearing my grandson as well now, which I don't regard as a tie in the sense that I wouldn't have anyone else doing it.

Farming does tie you down. It is not a job really. Everyone should understand that. It's a vocation. Not everyone wants to put on their wellingtons and their coat at twelve o'clock at night just as you are going to bed if there is a cow in labour in the shed. Women who have worked at something else outside farming probably would be slow to get involved. They have their pay packet at the end of the week and the weekend off, living a relatively normal life which you don't do on a farm. The people who really like that kind of life will do it and will continue to do it but quite a lot of the younger women work outside the farms at this moment in time. I think it's an economic necessity. The vast majority of farmers would prefer a good market price rather than subsidies. We're hoping all the time that it will improve down the road.

The vast majority of men still don't partake in housework to a large extent. It is always the women who deal with the school and the kids and that kind of thing. A lot of the women would be holding down jobs as well and I'd imagine that's still fairly typical. My husband helps out. He'll do the dinner on Saturday or Sunday if I'm doing my classwork or farmwork. That may not be typical. It's still traditional to some extent for the women to do the housework although in the twenty years that we've been back here things have changed considerably in that women go out more and are more involved in things. It is rare that you hear of a woman of farming background going to UCD to do agricultural science or something like that. If they do get a good education it is usually in some other field. You could say that farming is a sort of part-time occupation for most people around this vicinity. A lot of the women in farming would be working elsewhere.

There are a lot of social organisations in the place over the last fifteen years that weren't here before. A lot of it has to do with the local facilities. I'm studying towards a degree in English at the minute. UCC started an outreach programme around the year 2000 in Cahirciveen and the subject was English so we have been doing it in bits and pieces since then. There are about twenty people of varying ages in the Cahirciveen vicinity and another twenty in Kenmare. We also did Greek and Roman History. At the moment I'm doing an introductory course in archaeology in Teach Amergin in Waterville. I'm doing that this winter because there are credits available so I'm trying to build up my credits. We need 180 credits to get the degree. I love it. It's something I always wanted to do and didn't get the opportunity when I was young.

'I had good Irish and then I lived in the Gaeltacht in Mayo, Galway and Baile Bhúirne. Tá sí go líofa agam. A bhfuil de Ghaelainn i mo chuimhne anois ní úsáidim go minic í. I'm trying to teach Jack, my grandson. I think that's the important thing, getting the basics of it in the early years... I'd hate to think of a language that old dying out.'

This is a Breac-Ghaeltacht. I grew up with Irish. It wasn't the language of our home but I think my parents appreciated it. I think the emigration hit it badly around here as well. The school is a Gaeltacht school and most kids would speak Irish at school. Some of them who are really interested go on to the

Aonad Lán-Ghaelach in Cahirciveen. I had good Irish and then I lived in the Gaeltacht in Mayo, Galway and Baile Bhúirne. Tá sí go líofa agam. A bhfuil de Ghaolainn i mo chuimhne anois ní úsáidim go minic í. I'm trying to teach Jack, my grandson. I think that's the important thing, getting the basics of it in the early years. I can't see us as a bilingual country but I'd like to visualise a day when people would be at ease with it. There's so much agro where Irish is concerned, which I can understand. A lot of my generation especially in the cities had a tough time. I'm not sure about the compulsion aspect of it. I don't know what the happy medium is. I'd hate to think of a language that old dying out.

Sunday night is the big night locally. There is usually music and people dancing. It's not my scene really but the kids have always been involved in music. I like literature. I'll read anything from *Woman's Weekly* to the *Kerryman* or the daily paper. I've actually read *Ulysses* which I'm very proud of. I've listened to it all on tape. I bought a Walkman and I listen to it while I'm walking or if I'm in the car. I try to keep up with the bestsellers. I'm looking forward to reading the one that won the Booker prize recently, Anne Enright's *The Gathering*. I'll try to read anything that's topical. Almost every day you lift the paper a new book by a new writer is being reviewed which I find fantastic. I don't think I have any talent in that line but I'm quite happy to read other people's stories.